GOD'S
MAGNIFIED WORD

Volume IV,

Studies in Abundant Living

Victor Paul Wierwille

American Christian Press
The Way International
New Knoxville, Ohio 45871

Other books by Victor Paul Wierwille

Power for Abundant Living
Receiving the Holy Spirit Today
Are the Dead Alive Now?
The Bible Tells Me So
   Volume I, Studies in Abundant Living
The New, Dynamic Church
   Volume II, Studies in Abundant Living
The Word's Way
   Volume III, Studies in Abundant Living
Jesus Christ Is Not God

Standard Book Number ISBN 0-910068-13-5
Library of Congress Catalog Number 77-87405
American Christian Press
The Way International
New Knoxville, Ohio 45871
© 1977 by The Way International. All rights reserved
Second printing. Paperback
Printed in the United States of America

To my fellow
Board of Trustees
brothers

Ermal L. Owens
and
Harry Ernst Wierwille

For their faithfulness and
dedication as
vice-president and
secretary-treasurer
during the founding years of
The Way Ministry International

CONTENTS

Preface

God's Magnified Word is organized into four
parts: "God's Abundant Goodness," "A Believer's
Walk," "God's Strength in Us," "The Greatness of
the Church of Grace." Within each part are chapters,
each chapter having been researched and originally
written as an individual study. By loosely grouping
the chapters under general topics, a reader can get
a broader overview as the parts fit together to make
up the larger whole.

However, because the chapters were written as
individual studies and then grouped into topical
units, a reader may find that all facets of the topic
are not covered. More information may be sought
in other writings published by The American Christian Press, though more exhaustive research and
writing, no doubt, still need to be done on all topics.
In the meantime, I know that the contents of Volume IV of "Studies in Abundant Living" will not
only unveil more of God's Word for you, but, in
doing so, will also uplift you—mentally and physically
and spiritually.

Let us put God's Word in our hearts and minds, for
it alone can give us complete deliverance and dispel
the darkness of this world.

Part I

God's Abundant Goodness

Part I
God's Abundant Goodness

Throughout God's Word are constant examples and promises of abundance which God has made available to us, His children. One great key to abundant living involves a person's ability to rest. "A Rest to God's People" shows that God Himself established the precedent of resting when He did so on the seventh day, after ending His work on the sixth day. God provides special ways for us, His children, to rest and thereby have great endurance and peace.

"The Benefits of God" expounds the gem-filled one hundred and third psalm. This psalm unfolds a knowledge of God and encourages our humble praise and thanks to Him for being so understanding and so abundantly good to us.

In the third chapter, "Job: From Victim to Victor," we see the stark contrast of the prosperity of possessions, family, and health which God wants for His

1

own, juxtaposed with the destitution that Satan can inflict on man. Satan made a shambles of Job's life. Yet, out of the ash heap of Job's dilemma, God reversed Job's circumstances and marvelously delivered him.

God's love and abundance are manifold. How edifying it is to know of God's abundant goodness. What peace of mind and strength of believing we can gain from this knowledge of God and the promises of His matchless Word.

CHAPTER ONE

A Rest to God's People

One great key to successful living revolves around a person's ability to rest: to relax, to feel composed and assured. Capable athletes, such as boxers, must know how to roll with the punches. A man running in a race must know how to pace himself. People who play football must learn how to unpile slowly so that they get some needed rest before they get back into the huddle. A successful, long-lived business or professional person also has to be able to "live restfully." He has to learn to have confidence and ease when he is engaged in the enormous responsibilities and activities that are heaped upon him.

According to Genesis 2:2, when God had finished all of His works, it says, "And on the seventh day*

---

*The Samaritan Pentateuch and the Septuagint read "sixth day." Also, see Exodus 20:9 and 10: "Six days shalt thou labour, and do all thy work: But the seventh day *is* the sabbath of the Lord thy God: *in it* thou shalt not do any work, thou, nor thy son, nor thy daughter, thy manservant, nor thy maidservant, nor thy cattle, nor thy stranger that *is* within thy gates."

God ended his work which he had made; and he rested...." Hebrews 4:4 says, about the same event, "For he spake in a certain place of the seventh *day* on this wise, And God did rest the seventh day from all his works." In this same context we find in Hebrews a tremendous truth of God that we need to claim for ourselves.

Hebrews 4:9:
There remaineth therefore a rest to the people of God.

"There remaineth therefore a rest to the people of God." This is the secret to peaceful living; yet, very, very few Christians know the reality and the depth of this "rest." In the Book of I Kings, God talks about this rest for a whole nation.

I Kings 8:56:
Blessed *be* the Lord, that hath given rest unto his people Israel [to the whole nation], according to all that he promised: there hath not failed one word of all his good promise, which he promised by the hand of Moses his servant.

God did not fail on even one Word of His promises, and the promise here was that the whole nation of Israel should have rest. That is how God blessed His people.

God also promised rest to an entire city if they would return to His Word. For to Jerusalem, God said, there is "the good way, and walk therein, and ye shall find rest."

> Jeremiah 6:16:
> Thus saith the Lord, Stand ye [inhabitants of Jerusalem] in the ways, and see, and ask for the old paths, where *is* the good way, and walk therein, and ye shall find rest for your souls. But they said, We will not walk *therein.*

At one time Israel as a nation found rest; God also promised rest to the city of Jerusalem when He spoke that there "...is the good way, and walk therein, and ye shall find rest...." However, the people by their own volition determined not to walk according to God's Word and, therefore, they were denied the promised rest.

There is another rest in the Word, and that is the rest found in a marital relationship. Naomi said to her daughters-in-law Orpha and Ruth as recorded in Ruth 1:9, "The Lord grant you that ye may find rest, each *of you* in the house of her husband." Ruth did just that when she married Boaz. So there can be rest in married life.

In the gospel period, Jesus Christ promised rest to those who would be his disciples.

Matthew 11:28 and 29:
Come unto me, all *ye* that labour and are
heavy laden, and I will give you rest.
Take my yoke upon you, and learn of me;
for I am meek and lowly in heart: and ye shall
find rest unto your souls.

"Come unto me...and I will give you rest...ye
shall find rest unto your souls." Another great
promise of rest is found in the Book of Psalms.

Psalms 37:4-7:
Delight thyself also in the Lord; and he shall
give thee the desires of thine heart.
Commit thy way unto the Lord; trust also in
him; and he shall bring *it* to pass.
And he shall bring forth thy righteousness as
the light, and thy judgment as the noonday.
Rest in the Lord, and wait patiently for him:
fret not thyself because of him who prospereth
in his way, because of the man who bringeth
wicked devices to pass.

Don't pay any attention to those who appear to
prosper in their own ways, but rest in the Lord and
wait patiently for Him. That is the great key to rest-
ful living. We cannot be conditioned by the people
and situations surrounding us and still expect to
find rest. Looking at the Lord and waiting patiently

6

for Him, delighting ourselves in the Lord, committing our ways to Him, trusting in Him—this gives us rest.

God, after He had finished His creation, rested. The word "rest" means the same as the word "sat." Why do people sit? To rest. When God had finished His works, He rested, He sat. Everything was finished. When Jesus Christ had finished his work for us, he ascended into heaven and sat down.* The believer's right to rest is a result of the finished work of Christ. When Christ had finished his work, he sat down on the right hand of God because all had been completed for man—for those who choose to believe.

Another great usage of "sat" occurs when the day of Pentecost was fully come. Acts 2:3 says that the gift of the holy spirit was given "...and it [holy spirit] sat upon each of them [the twelve apostles]." The fulfillment of all requirements toward the giving of the holy spirit to those who believe had been completely completed and, therefore, it sat, rested, on each of them.

This secret to living restfully is embodied within Christ's finished work for the believer. We know that we are what God says we are, that we have what

---

*Hebrews 10:12: "But this man [Jesus Christ], after he had offered one sacrifice for sins for ever, sat down on the right hand of God." See also Hebrews 1:3, Ephesians 1:20, and Romans 8:34.

God's Abundant Goodness

He says we have, that we will be what He says we will be. We know that we have passed from death unto life. We know that we are a part of the family of God, the Body of Christ. We know that we have been circumcised with Christ, we have been baptized with him, we have been buried with him, we have been raised together with him. When he ascended, according to the Word of God, we ascended with him and are seated with him at the right hand of God.* This is why we have a life which is more abundant. This is why we can have great restfulness.

With this knowledge of God's Word in our lives, we have really reached the end of our struggles; the end of all fear, worry, and anxiety because we have full knowledge that God is our all in all. When God looks at us, He sees us as one with Him because of what Christ wrought: God in Christ in us. You and I have entered into that rest spiritually by what Jesus Christ did for us. Now it becomes a part of our lives as we literally walk upon that Word and claim those promises which are ours. Look at the confidence we have if we walk according to the advice of Philippians.

*Ephesians 2:5 and 6: "Even when we were dead in sins, hath quick-ened us together with Christ, (by grace ye are saved;)
And hath raised *us* up together, and made *us* sit together in heavenly *places* in Christ Jesus."

Philippians 4:6:
Be careful [The word "careful" should be translated "anxious." Be anxious] for nothing; but in every thing by prayer and supplication with thanksgiving let your requests be made known unto God.

We have no anxiety when we live in the knowledge of what Christ accomplished for us. The next verse in Philippians 4 continues to encourage us.

Philippians 4:7:
And the peace of God, which passeth all understanding, shall [absolutely] keep your hearts and minds through Christ Jesus.

Isn't that a beautiful rest? That is the secret of living serenely. Spiritually we *are* what the Word of God says we are and we *have* what the Word of God says we have. Christ paid for it; he purchased it. Then why do we so frequently see Christians who are nervous, frustrated, and full of fear? Because they have not learned the secret of living, the secret of resting in that rest which is already theirs and was paid for by Christ Jesus. When we have confidence in the promises of God because of the accomplishments of Christ Jesus, we have the peace of God in our hearts and minds.

9

God's Abundant Goodness

When we believe on the Lord Jesus Christ, he takes his abode within us. And then by our application of the Word, we can live in him: he in us; and we in him. As we speak God's Word, it becomes living and real in our lives. As we believe God's Word, it comes into concretion. Practicing God's Word brings peace into fruition in our lives.

> I Peter 5:7:
> Casting all your care upon him; for he careth for you.

This verse says, "Casting all...." And the word "all" means *all*. Trusting God's Word is so simple, but the Adversary tries to talk us out of it. Satan keeps doing his utmost to keep us from believing the totality of the word "all." And he does this so stealthily that we aren't aware of what's happening until our lives are frayed and threadbare.

> I Peter 5:8:
> Be sober, be vigilant; because your adversary the devil, as a roaring lion, walketh about, seeking whom he may devour.

Once you and I have entered into God's rest, then no longer can we be disturbed by the roaring of the Adversary. We have cast our care upon God. The Adversary is just roaring, and he cannot bite when

10

he is roaring. The reason he makes a loud, ferocious racket is to frighten us, to freeze us in our tracks so that he can then pounce. But we are no longer to be disturbed by the roar of what people say. The questions our best friends may ask no longer upset us. The doubts that other people have about God and His Word don't rattle us, because we are in His rest. We have arrived at the place that we trust God's Word. This is why we are no longer circumstance-conditioned; we are God's Word-conditioned. Most people go through life being conditioned by their circumstances—by people, places, things. So one day they feel as lighthearted as can be and the next day they are moody and melancholy. The people who are perfectly conditioned by God's Word have an even, steady assurance and peacefulness.

Now a different scripture to fit into the context of this study on rest is Philippians 4:11.

> Not that I speak in respect of want: for I have learned, in whatsoever state I am, *therewith* to be content.

That is the King James rendition, and it is erroneous. This verse conveys the idea that, for example, if you are sick, you should just enjoy being sick—be content and at peace with your condition. If you are dying, be content that you are dying. If someone runs

11

over your foot and smashes it with a tractor, be content. No, No! You see, this teaching that you have to be content with suffering is just a trick of the Adversary. How can you have confidence and feel rested when you're miserable? God does not need the Adversary to help make your life and mine complete. We've got something far better in Christ Jesus. The accurate text of Philippians 4:11 reads: "Not that I speak in respect of want; for I have learned in whatsoever state I am, I am self-sufficient, self-adequate." What a tremendous revelation! We are self-adequate. Why? Because God made us adequate. That is why circumstances do not condition us. God made us adequate and sufficient—and God should know. Look at the next two verses in Philippians 4.

> Verses 12 and 13:
> [In my self-adequacy] I [Paul] know both how to be abased, and I know how to abound: every where and in all things I am instructed both to be full and to be hungry, both to abound and to suffer need.
> I can do all things [I can do them because I am in that rest; I have learned the secret of living.] through Christ which [who] strengtheneth me.

The Amplified Bible translates verse 13 as follows: "I am ready for anything and equal to anything through him who infuses inner strength into me

12

[that is, I am self-sufficient in Christ's sufficiency]."
Our ability comes from an infusion; it is a spiritual
intravenous feeding: Christ in us the hope of glory.
That is quality spiritual strengthening, isn't it? Why
do we need this infusion?

> Colossians 1:10:
> That ye might walk worthy of the Lord unto
> all pleasing, being fruitful in every good work,
> and increasing in the knowledge of God.

We walk worthy of the Lord by being fruitful—not
only fruitful, but increasing in that knowledge of
God. The more knowledge of God's Word we have,
the more fruitful in every good work we can become.
The knowledge of the Word and its application will
produce fruit. By conditioning our minds to God's
Word and walking in its truth, we enter into great
rest. This rest is a result of believing the integrity
of God's wonderful, matchless Word. What a magnificent reality. Truly, there remains a rest to God's
people when we cast our cares upon Him, when we
are anxious for nothing, when we accept what God
through Christ Jesus has given us.

CHAPTER TWO

The Benefits of God

Psalms 103 is a tremendous example of knowledge and praise. Just the reading of it thrills the heart of anyone who loves God. The beauty with which this is set just from a human point of view, without even thinking of its spiritual impact, should set at peace the soul of any man or woman. For us as born-again believers there are tremendous spiritual truths hidden in this psalm that will elevate and enrich our lives as we learn them.

PSALMS 103

Bless the Lord, O my soul: and all that is within me, *bless* his holy name.

Bless the Lord, O my soul, and forget not all his benefits:

Who forgiveth all thine iniquities; who healeth all thy diseases;

Who redeemeth thy life from destruction; who crowneth thee with lovingkindness and tender mercies;

Who satisfieth thy mouth with good *things;*
so that thy youth is renewed like the eagle's.

The Lord executeth righteousness and judgment
for all that are oppressed.

He made known his ways unto Moses, his acts
unto the children of Israel.

The Lord *is* merciful and gracious, slow to anger,
and plenteous in mercy.

He will not always chide: neither will he keep
his anger for ever.

He hath not dealt with us after our sins; nor
rewarded us according to our iniquities.

For as the heaven is high above the earth, *so*
great is his mercy toward them that fear him.

As far as the east is from the west, *so* far hath
he removed our transgressions from us.

Like as a father pitieth *his* children, *so* the
Lord pitieth them that fear him.

For he knoweth our frame; he remembereth
that we *are* dust.

As for man, his days *are* as grass: as a flower
of the field, so he flourisheth.

For the wind passeth over it, and it is gone;
and the place thereof shall know it no more.

But the mercy of the Lord *is* from everlasting
to everlasting upon them that fear him, and his
righteousness unto children's children;

To such as keep his covenant, and to those that

remember his commandments to do them.

The Lord hath prepared his throne in the heavens; and his kingdom ruleth over all.

Bless the Lord, ye his angels [messengers, ministers], that excel in strength, that do his commandments, hearkening unto the voice of his word.

Bless ye the Lord, all *ye* his hosts; *ye* ministers of his, that do his pleasure.

Bless the Lord, all his works in all places of his dominion: bless the Lord, O my soul.

To understand the richness of this psalm, let's look at it verse by verse.

Verses 1 and 2:

Bless the Lord, O my soul: and all that is within me, *bless* his holy name.

Bless the Lord, O my soul, and forget not all his benefits.

With my whole being, I want to bless the Lord and bless His holy name. And let me not forget all His benefits. Wouldn't it be too overwhelming if verse 2 said, "Bless the Lord, O my soul, and remember all His benefits"? Which one of us could possibly begin to remember and then enumerate all the blessings, all the benefits, that we have received from God through the years? None of us could. Therefore, in this tremendous psalm God does not tell us to remember all the benefits; He simply asks us not to forget them all. "Bless the Lord, O my soul, and forget not all his benefits." There are certainly some times that we can remember when He has benefited us. He has called us out of darkness into the marvelous light of the gospel of redemption and salvation; He has made His Word living and real to us; He has taught us the keys that are so beautifully written in His Word such as, His Word is His will. How tremendous it is to just not forget what we were at one time and what He has made us today. What joy it is to realize the grace with which God has taken and loved us with an everlasting love, putting His hand on us to somehow bring us into a life that many of us would have considered impossible. We have had answers to prayer; we have had the privilege of ministering to people and seeing God's mighty deliverance performed in their lives; we have seen people's lives changed when we have taught them the Word of God, when this Word of God again started to make sense to them as they saw how beautifully it fits together.

"Bless the Lord, O my soul, and forget not all his benefits." Just think of a few of them and your heart will bubble with thanksgiving. The enthusiasm within your soul of knowing that God has wrought these things within your life will indeed inspire you to "bless His holy name." How blessed we are!

Verse 3:
Who forgiveth all thine iniquities [sins]...

Now there are many people who believe the first part of this verse, but somehow when they get to the second part they begin to doubt.

...who healeth all thy diseases.

Now logically, if any one person has a right to scratch out a part of a verse in the Word of God, then every person has a right to scratch out whatever he chooses. But, when one person deletes or negates one verse and someone else deletes another verse, we no longer have the Word of God. It is either all God's Word or it isn't. It is as simple as all that. Just because one verse or passage does not agree with your or my theology does not invalidate it or make it any less God's Word. It is not a question of whether the truth of God's Word agrees with our theology; it is a question of whether or not we agree with God's Word.

Verse 3 of Psalms 103 very plainly says, "Who forgiveth all thine iniquities; who healeth all [without exception] thy diseases." Does God forgive your

18

sins? Well then, does God heal you? He must or He is a liar; but God is no liar. People may then question, "Well, why doesn't God heal everybody?" Healing for all is God's will. But when we fail to rise up to our rightful and legal privileges, due to a variety of causes—the greatest cause being a negative society where people talk about, expect, and cope with negative things—we fail to be healed. To claim and manifest God's healing we must believe on the positives of His Word, not the negatives of the world. If we would become immersed in the Word and start living, we would find that God is still able to quiet down the nerves; God is still able to bring health and peace without antibiotics, sedatives, or alcohol.

Verse 4:
Who redeemeth thy life from destruction....

God redeems us from the destruction that is constantly around to destroy us. Do you get the impact of this truth? That which surrounds us every day, that which endeavors to kill us prematurely— God has redeemed our lives from that type of destruction. And He adds to this safeness the warmth and love which makes life enjoyable.

Verses 4b and 5a:
...who crowneth thee with lovingkindness and [by His] tender mercies.
Who satisfieth thy [your] mouth with good *things*....

We are redeemed from a life of destruction, from a life of negatives—the frustrations, the fears, the anxieties. He redeems us from this. Then He crowns us with lovingkindness and tender mercies and satisfies our mouths with *good* things. This is a tremendous difference from what some people have in their mouths. Some have all negatives while others have positives. And when you meet the second type, the moment they shake your hand you sense their goodness and soundness.

Verse 5:
Who satisfieth thy mouth with good *things;* *so that* thy youth is renewed like the eagle's.

Here God's Word is not talking about Ponce de Leon's fountain of youth in Florida. If you are 75, you cannot believe to be 20. God set up the law of time. Therefore, once you are 21, you cannot go back to being 20 in the physical sense because that is a natural law. He established that law of time, but He also set the spiritual law. This is in the context of this tremendous psalm containing the wonderful spiritual truth, "...thy youth is renewed like the eagle's." This expression means that, no matter how old you are, you can constantly have youthful vigor and maintain that mental aliveness; you are not burdened down with the negatives of other people of the same age. Young people are vivacious; they feel as though they can conquer the world, as though they can trounce on any problem.

Until Bishop K.C. Pillai from India taught the greatness of this renewing of youth like the eagle's, this figure of speech didn't make sense to me. What does the eagle have which renews its strength, and how does that relate to us? Well, this passage refers to an eagle found in the Orient. This kind of eagle will periodically soar to tremendous heights, and then suddenly, it will fold its wings under, head straight down, and bomb into the sea with as much speed as it can generate. When the eagle surfaces, it hasn't any feathers on its back, so must float back to shore and crawl in among the bushes until its feathers have grown out. Isn't that something!

God renews our youth like the eagle's. He renews our youth by enabling us to get rid of all our ballast— all those old, dirty feathers, all those negatives, those fears, those worries, those anxieties, all of the things that have burdened us down.

This renewal like an eagle's is a benefit we should not forget. "...Forget not all his benefits...." Think about how God has enabled us to drop off those things that at one time disturbed us and, in many cases, overcame us. It must be as the Apostle Paul wrote in Philippians 3:13 and 14: "...Forgetting those things which are behind, and reaching forth unto those things which are before, I press toward the mark...." Forgetting the things which are behind is the same general truth written in this psalm: "*so that* thy youth is renewed like the eagle's."

> Verses 6 and 7:
> The Lord executeth righteousness and judgment for all that are oppressed.
> He made known his ways unto Moses, his acts unto the children of Israel.

Isn't that terrific! Have you read in the Old Testament how God worked with Moses? Aaron was given to Moses to be Moses' mouthpiece. So God gave information to Moses, who in turn told Aaron, who in turn told Pharaoh and the children of Israel. "He [God] made known his ways unto Moses...." With a careful reading of the Old Testament, we note that God told Moses why He did certain things, what His purposes were, His intents. But God never fully explained Himself to the children of Israel. He made known His ways unto Moses, but all that the children

of Israel ever saw were the acts of God. They believed
God because of the acts they saw and not because
God went around explaining His actions to them.

Verses 8-10:
The Lord *is* merciful and gracious, slow to
anger, and plenteous in mercy.
He will not always chide: neither will he keep
his anger for ever (The figure of speech is
anthropopatheia, attributing to God the human
characteristic of anger.).
He hath not dealt with us after our sins; nor
rewarded us according to our iniquities.

This verse ten contains another figure of speech
exergasia. Here we have the same expression stated
in two different ways which establishes the truth
as unchangeable.* God does not deal with us according to our sins which also includes that He does not
reward us according to our iniquities. That truth
is established.

Verses 11 and 12:
For as the heaven is high above the earth, *so*
great is his mercy toward them that fear him
[who have respect for Him, who love Him, who
have awe for Him].

*Genesis 41:32: "And for that the dream was doubled unto Pharaoh
twice; *it is* because the thing *is* established by God, and God will
shortly bring it to pass."

As far as the east is from the west, *so* far hath he removed our transgressions [sins, iniquities] from us.

How far is the east from the west? Do you know that the east *never* meets the west? That cannot be said of north and south. People, when we begin to tell the greatness of God's Word and understand the way in which God dealt with us when He gave us remission and forgiveness of sins, then we cannot help but be thankful to be alive and to be a part of God's love and wonderful power today. God is merciful beyond measure to those who respect Him.

Verses 13 and 14:
Like as a father pitieth *his* children, *so* the Lord pitieth [loveth] them that fear [awe, respect] him.
For he knoweth our frame; he remembereth that we *are* dust.

Thank God He does remember our dust. It would be miserable if He didn't remember and understand us. Had God not known us, He never would have instituted the means by which Christ had ultimately to come to redeem us and give us victory in our lives. God knows our frame. He knows that we are like grass. He knows that the wind passes over and the place thereof remembers it no more.

Verses 15-19:
As for man, his days *are* as grass: as a flower of
the field, so he flourisheth.
For the wind passeth over it, and it is gone;
and the place thereof shall know it no more.
But the mercy of the Lord *is* from everlasting
to everlasting upon them that fear him, and
his righteousness unto children's children;
To such as keep his covenant, and to those that
remember his commandments to do them.
The Lord hath prepared his throne in the
heavens; and his kingdom [God's kingdom]
ruleth over all.

God will have the ultimate say. He is the one who
has the final pronouncement. And His mercy abounds
to those that keep His commandments, His Word.

Then comes this powerful twentieth verse.

Verse 20:
Bless the Lord, ye his angels [messengers],
that excel in strength, that do his commandments, hearkening unto the voice of his word.

These verses talk about how God has redeemed us,
how He has cast our sin from us as far as the east is
from the west, and that He has prepared His throne.

25

His kingdom rules over all. Therefore, "Bless the Lord, ye his messengers [not angels, but people who speak His Word] that excel in strength...." *Our* excelling in strength comes with our having cast off all those things which have held us back; then with singleness of mind we have set our sights on the things of God and moved forth with the greatness of His Word. That is why we excel in strength. It is His strength in us. Another scripture, Philippians 4:13, corroborates this by saying, "I can do all things through Christ which [who] strengtheneth me." God's strength in Christ in us is our strength.

> Verses 21 and 22:
> Bless ye the Lord, all *ye* his hosts; *ye* ministers of his, that do his pleasure.
> Bless the Lord, all his works in all places of his dominion: bless the Lord, O my soul.

When we know the greatness of God's Word and of His works, when we know that this Word of God is accurate and life-giving, there is nothing to do but to say, "Bless the Lord for His incomparable greatness. I have not forgotten all His benefits to me. I thank Him for forgiving my shortcomings and for healing all my diseases. It is God who has crowned me with lovingkindness and tender mercies in place of the world's destruction; it is God who has satisfied my mouth with good things and given me the renewed life of a youth. All God's messengers, all God's ministers, all God's hosts, all God's works in all places of God's dominion praise His name. Bless the Lord, O my soul." What a positive, uplifting psalm. How thankful and blessed we are when we consider God as the great psalmist did.

CHAPTER THREE

Job: From Victim to Victor

God's Goodness
vs.
The Devil's Badness

There are many passages in the Bible on healing, but there is only one book that deals with human suffering and healing. That book is the Book of Job.

The story of Job is a drama. It is a true story: the story of men's lives—such as your life and mine. No one sojourns in life for a long period of time until he or she experiences at least a portion of the emotions and pain expressed in the account of Job. Job's story moves from suffering to believing to deliverance.

The Book of Job gives us, in detailed form, a striking comparison between the goodness of God and the badness of the Devil. We see vividly the true color of Satan. Job starkly shows what happens to every man when Satan has his way.

Job is the man in whose life the will of God is manifested at times, and the power of Satan at other times. In this account we see God as He really is to His children. We see God's great goodness, His absolute will, His supreme love. Then, also, we see a true picture of Satan: the poverty to which he reduces men, his hate, his complete evil.

God had the account of Job recorded for one major purpose: to show us the goodness of God and the badness of the Devil; to show us the perfection of God and the wickedness of the Devil; to show us that God is all good and that the Devil is all bad. God desires all men to see His will, in contrast to the Devil's will.

In the first chapter of this book, Job is blessed as God wanted him to be having those things which God desires for all believers.

Job 1:1:
...Job...was perfect and upright, and one that feared God, and eschewed evil.

This word "perfect" means faultless. In the sight of God, Job walked perfectly according to God's will. "Upright" means moral integrity. Job, because of his relationship with God, was an upright man. The statement "perfect and upright" is a figure of speech called *hendiadys,* which would literally be stated as "uprightly perfect." Job feared God, which means he

29

had great reverence, respect, and awe for God. Because Job feared God, he "eschewed [shunned] evil"; even all appearances of evil were distasteful to him.

> Job 1:2:
> ...there were born unto him [Job] seven sons and three daughters.

God's plan for man is that he should have a prosperous family life, that he be blessed with a good wife and loving children. When a man loves God, when he really knows and honors Him, his family is blessed.

> Job 1:3:
> His [Job's] substance also was seven thousand sheep, and three thousand camels, and five hundred yoke of oxen, and five hundred she asses, and a very great household; so that this man was the greatest of all the men of the east.

God's will for His people is prosperity and abundance, that all men may know and see God's blessing exemplified. Job was a God-fearing man, and, because he revered and served God and believed for an abundance, God poured out these material blessings upon him. The will of God is always abundance for His believing people. God's will is specifically stated in III John 2: "Beloved, I wish above all things that thou mayest prosper and be in health, even as thy soul prospereth." And the psalmist observed how God cares for the righteous in Psalms 37:25: "I have been young, and *now* am old; yet have I not seen the righteous forsaken, nor his seed begging bread." God's will is an abundance of prosperity and blessings unlimited for His children.

Job 1:4:
And his sons went and feasted *in their* houses, every one his day....

Every one of Job's sons had a house to live in. God was pleased that Job believed for all these possessions and that Job's sons were so richly blessed as well. It is God's will for people to have blessings. God is good and His goodness is to be manifested. Most people think that the more spiritual a man becomes, the less joy and pleasure he has in life. This is not true when God has His way.

Satan's comments about Job's condition were very accurate.

Job 1:10:
Hast not thou [God] made an hedge about him [Job], and about his house, and about all that he hath on every side? thou hast blessed the

31

work of his hands, and his substance is increased in the land.

This is an accurate analysis of the goodness and will of God for men. Notice, God had put a hedge around Job. Why shouldn't God put a hedge around believers? It is His will for His people to be protected; it is God's will for people to have goodness; it is His will for people to have the power of God in their lives. When we belong to God, we should expect God's hedge to be around us for our complete protection from the Devil and his acts. God makes a hedge available for the life of every believer; but the impenetrability of the hedge is dependent upon our believing the promises of His Word.

God is always good; God never brings evil. There is absolutely no darkness in God; no sickness, no poverty, no deficiency. God does not want His people afflicted, miserable, poor, unhappy, or defeated. All the blessings that came to Job were abundance from God, because Job loved and respected Him. When God's will was operative in Job, his life was abundant. God wants all good for all His children: health, prosperity, happiness, and abundance.

Now let us note the description of the Devil.

Job 1:6 and 7:
Now there was a day when the sons of God
came to present themselves before the Lord,
and Satan came also among them.
And the Lord said unto Satan, Whence comest
thou? Then Satan answered the Lord, and said,
From going to and fro in the earth, and from
walking up and down in it.

God is everywhere present at all times; the Devil
is not. The Devil is only present at certain times.
His place of habitation is the earth.

Job 1:9:
Then Satan answered the Lord, and said, Doth
Job fear God for nought?

We just read of God's goodness flowing from God
to Job; now Satan comes along and starts interjecting
questions. Next Satan will try to tempt God.

Job 1:11:
But [you, God,] put forth thine hand now,
and touch all that he [Job] hath, and he will
curse thee to thy face.

God always puts His blessing on believers and the
Devil is always trying to take away man's blessing.
God's will is abundance; the Devil's will is poverty

33

and destruction. People sometimes say, "God sent a sickness or disease or calamity." This is not true; the Devil sends it. Note what the Devil will do to a man if he can; note his true intent and desire.

One day when Job's sons and daughters were happy and enjoying life, Satan, not God, brought destruction.

Job 1:13-19:

And there was a day when his sons and his daughters *were* eating and drinking wine in their eldest brother's house:

And there came a messenger unto Job, and said, The oxen were plowing, and the asses feeding beside them:

And the Sabeans fell *upon them,* and took them away; yea, they have slain the servants with the edge of the sword; and I only am escaped alone to tell thee.

While he *was* yet speaking, there came also another, and said, The fire of God is fallen from heaven, and hath burned up the sheep, and the servants, and consumed them; and I only am escaped alone to tell thee.

While he *was* yet speaking, there came also another, and said, the Chaldeans made out three bands, and fell upon the camels, and have carried them away, yea, and slain the servants with the edge of the sword; and I only am escaped alone to tell thee.

While he *was* speaking, there came also another, and said, Thy sons and thy daughters *were* eating and drinking wine in their eldest brother's house:

And, behold, there came a great wind from the wilderness, and smote the four corners of the house, and it fell upon the young men, and they were dead; and I only am escaped alone to tell thee.

Note that the Devil worked through people as well as the natural elements. He used the Sabeans and the Chaldeans and the wind. The Devil may work through your best friend, through your neighbor, or through any other person to assert himself in your life and take away from you what God has given you.

Wouldn't you agree that all Job's losses were too much for one man to endure? The Devil is never satisfied until he has reduced man to complete nothingness. Yet even after all these losses for Job, Satan's true and full colors had not yet been completely displayed.

Job 2:7:
So went Satan forth from the presence of the Lord, and smote Job with sore boils from the sole of his foot unto his crown.

Who smote Job? Satan did. Satan covered Job with boils.

Job left the place where he was living and walked out to a little ash heap. He sat down upon the ash heap, took a potsherd, and scraped himself.*

Job was miserable from head to foot both mentally and physically because of Satan's workings. Yet, people try to make us believe that sickness is a blessing which will draw men closer to God or cause them to be better Christians. They say that it humbles one so he may become a more refined man of God. This is not what God's Word says. In the last chapter of the Book of Job, in Job 42:10, God calls sickness "captivity." What is captivity? It is enslavement, bondage, that which prevents a person from doing what one ought to be doing or what one wants to be doing. God called Job's sickness and disease "captivity," and we must call things by God's terms.

Once I was talking to a woman whose father had been sick for two and a half months, and she herself was a nervous wreck. "He can't turn over in bed because when he does the pain is like a knife in his

---

*The "ash heap" symbolizes utter penitence. A clay pot symbolizes divinity to the people of the Bible lands, thus they believe that scraping with a piece of a broken pot, a potsherd, will have a healing effect.

back. He can't endure taking a bath because his body is so tender," she said. You call that heaven? I would rather call it hell. Some may call it good; the Word calls it captivity.

If people say it is God's will for Christians to be poor, miserable, and afflicted, you must read the Book of Job to them. This Book of Job shows God's will manifested in Job's prosperity, happiness, peace, and joy. It was Satan, not God, who took away the prosperity, happiness, peace, and joy which Job once had.

God made Job the most prosperous man in all the East. Satan came and took all, leaving Job without family, without possessions, and without health. What a contrast! Job had been perfect and complete. Satan made Job to become imperfect and destitute.

Believing and Fear

According to the fifth verse of the first chapter of Job, Job feared that his children were not properly respecting God. Job was afraid that his children were sinning, that they might have separated themselves from God in their hearts, that they were not living as they ought to have been. So Job, in order to safeguard them, offered burnt offerings continually for every one of his children.

Job 1:5:
...Job sent and sanctified them, and rose up early in the morning, and offered burnt offerings *according* to the number of them [his children] all: for Job said, It may be that my sons have sinned, and cursed God in their hearts. Thus did Job continually.

Here we are told one of Job's fears. It is also the first clue we have to a hole in God's hedge around Job. Is fear so potent that one break in the hedge

39

was all Satan needed to get into Job's life to defeat him and to bring all of the power of evil upon Job? How detrimental is fear?

Fear, in psychological terms, is classified as an emotion. Psychology says that newborn children have only two fears: one is the fear of falling and the other is the fear of loud noises. Thus man's multiple fears are basically acquired or learned, not innate. Fears are obtained by the avenue of the five senses. If your child is afraid of the "boogy man," he has that fear because someone taught him wrongly. If your child has a fear of being deserted, someone has put that fear in your child by wrong teaching or bad treatment.

Fear works the same in your life and in my life as it did in Job's. Job sensed that his daughters and his sons were not living right with God, and what he *believed* brought that fear into his conscious life. Fear *is* believing—negative believing. Job believed that the things he and his family possessed were too good to last. Job received the results of his negative believing. So it was Job's fear that was the hole in God's hedge which gave Satan an opening through which he could enter and destroy Job.

If I have fear, that fear has not come from God but through my wrong believing. If I have fear, I have

40

listened to and believed Satan, for "...God hath not given us the spirit of fear...."* On the other hand, God makes positive believing so simple.

Fear is the product of negative believing; it is wrong thinking, wrong believing. In Mark 5:36 Jesus said, "...Be not afraid, only believe." If it be true that Christ is with you always, then why should you fear? When you fear, you are not believing God's Word.

Any man who believes God's words will be blessed. Positive believing, believing God, gives you the fulfillment of the promises of God for your life. But if a person believes the lies of the Devil, he is going to be full of fear and thus reap the corresponding results.

I dare not give Satan a chance to get into my mind and put those negative fears within me. Today, I make a positive confession. I confess what the Word says. I confess my believing in God and what He says, and then by my will I believe God's promises to me and fears disappear. Fears have brought nothing but ruin, defeat, and captivity. The moment we are afraid, Satan has already moved in. And when

*II Timothy 1:7: "For God hath not given us the spirit of fear; but of power, and of love, and of a sound mind."

41

he wiggles in through a break in the hedge and gets a toehold, it won't be long until he has a foothold.

We must believe rightly without fear of anything, knowing that with the Lord in your life nothing can harm you. We must know the Lord is with us as stated in Psalms 139:8: "...if I make my bed in hell, behold, thou *art there.*" We must expect to drive our automobiles and be safe. We must expect to go to our businesses and jobs without fear, because underneath us are the everlasting arms of God, on each side of us are the everlasting arms of God, and above us are the everlasting arms of God.

What was it the angel said to the shepherds on the Judean hills the night Jesus was born? "Fear not." What did the angel say who appeared to Mary, the mother of Jesus? "Fear not." Wherever God is and wherever the power of God is known, the message is "Fear not." Job got the result of his fearing.

Job 3:25:
For the thing which I greatly feared is come upon me, and that which I was afraid of is come unto me.

This verse should be in letters an inch high, for it unfolds the great law of believing. Whatever we are believing is how we are going to be living.

Proverbs 23:7:
...as he thinketh in his heart, so *is* he.

Jesus' words, "Be of good cheer," are recorded several times in the gospels. Literally, the meaning is "believe positively that which is right; be not afraid."

Mark 11:22-24:
And Jesus answering saith unto them, Have faith in God.
For verily I say unto you, That whosoever shall say unto this mountain, Be thou removed, and be thou cast into the sea; and shall not doubt in his heart, but shall believe that those things which he saith shall come to pass; he shall have whatsoever he saith.
Therefore I say unto you, What things soever ye desire, when ye pray, believe that ye receive *them*, and ye shall have *them*.

Have you been living in fear? Fear is wrong believing, not trusting the promises of God. You can live on positive believing if you will change your thinking patterns. You must do the changing by the renewing of your mind according to the promises in the Word of God.

```
┌─────────────────────────────────────┐
│             TO BELIEVE               │
│   NEGATIVE    │    POSITIVE          │
│    Doubt      │   Confidence         │
│    Worry      │     Trust            │
│     Fear      │     Faith            │
│  ISSUES IN    │   ISSUES IN          │
│   UNBELIEF    │   BELIEVING          │
└─────────────────────────────────────┘
```

Job was sick for a period of perhaps six months or so—not for years, as some people exaggerate. Notice that after Job was released from captivity, he lived a hundred and thirty years.

I know we are not perfect as far as physical perfection is concerned. We may at times have diseases, but these should not linger. When we say "I believe God's Word" and *really* believe it, we come out the victor. We will come out the same way Job came out—delivered.

Many people believe it is God who tries or tests men; but that is not what the Scriptures say.

James 1:13 and 14:
Let no man say when he is tempted, I am tempted of God: for God cannot be tempted

with evil, neither tempteth he any man:
But every man is tempted, when he is drawn
away of his own lust, and enticed.

We receive good from God and evil from the
hand of Satan. Whatever we have in life, we manifest
because of our believing.

God brings only blessings. It seems to take much
spiritual growth before people will accept the fact
that God is good, *always*. Remember that III John 2
says, "Beloved, I wish above all things that thou
mayest prosper and be in health, even as thy soul
prospereth." John 10:10 says, "...I am come that
they might have life, and that they might have
it more abundantly." And Psalms 37:4 says, "Delight thyself also in the Lord; and he shall give thee
the desires of thine heart."

It is God's will "...above all things"—for us to
prosper. Therefore, why not believe God's promise
of prosperity rather than fear Satan's poverty?
The prosperity of your substance and health is
dependent upon how much our minds are renewed
to what God's Word says.

Do you think things are too good for you? Do
you think God has been too good to you and blessed
you with too much? Has He opened the windows of

45

heaven too wide for you and you have received too many blessings? The Word says that you are supposed to prosper.

God wants you to have prosperity; Satan wants us to have nothing. Our believing—positive or negative—determines our condition. This is a law.

Miserable Comforters

Job 2:11-13:

Now when Job's three friends heard of all this evil that was come upon him, they came every one from his own place; Eliphaz the Temanite, and Bildad the Shuhite, and Zophar the Naamathite: for they had made an appointment together to come to mourn with him and to comfort him.

And when they lifted up their eyes afar off, and knew him not, they lifted up their voice, and wept; and they rent every one his mantle, and sprinkled dust upon their heads toward heaven.

So they sat down with him upon the ground seven days and seven nights, and none spake a word unto him: for they saw that *his* grief was very great.

Later in the record, Job called these three men, Eliphaz, Bildad, and Zophar, "miserable comforters."* The study of these three men in chapters four through forty is most enlightening. Note that when these three men, who were friends of Job, heard about his unhappy condition, they came to comfort him. So they sat down with him for seven days and seven nights without saying a word. This is an Oriental custom showing total sympathy in extreme distress. They sat on the ash heap with Job because they saw that his grief was overwhelming. These "miserable comforters" were well-meaning men. But yet a well-meaning person can still be wrong. Note something else about Eliphaz, Bildad, and Zophar: they spoke great truths at various places in the Book of Job, but not truth for the given situation. After Satan brought all this destruction and sickness, he endeavored, by using Job's intimate friends, to bring more evil to Job. We see that the Devil frequently uses those whom we think of as our best friends to aggravate our conditions. The Devil is wily.

Note that in the New Testament when the Devil tempted Jesus, he quoted scripture. The portions of scripture the Devil quoted were true enough, but he removed them from their context. Whenever the

---

*Job 16:1 and 2: "Then Job answered and said, I have heard many such things: miserable comforters *are* ye all."

Devil uses truth, he always twists, manipulates it. Likewise, Job's three friends who came to comfort him spoke truths, but not the truth regarding Job's particular situation.

Eliphaz spoke first in Job 4:5.

> But now it [Job's dilemma] is come upon thee, and thou faintest; it toucheth thee, and thou art troubled.

Eliphaz reproved Job. He said, "Job, you are a wonderful man, but now since this trouble has come upon you, you cannot take it." God is judging you, friend Job, so you had better repent and get right with Him. This was the attitude of Eliphaz.

> Job 4:6 and 7:
> *Is* not *this* thy fear, thy confidence, thy hope, and the uprightness of thy ways?
> Remember, I pray thee, who *ever* perished, being innocent? or where were the righteous cut off?

"Job, can you show me that there was ever a man who perished who was innocent, or where the righteous men were cut off?" This passage of scripture sounds like truth, but Eliphaz inaccurately interpreted it.

Job was faultless, he eschewed evil. Did he perish? I should say not. These men thought they knew the reason, but the final outcome had not yet been recorded. When the end came, the Lord broke Job's bands of the captivity.

Job again spoke in chapter seven.

> Job 7:4:
> When I lie down, I say, When shall I arise, and the night be gone? and I am full of tossings to and fro unto the dawning of the day.

I point out this verse to you because so many people say that sickness is a blessing of God, that it is the Lord's will. The night has unending hours in it for the sick. When is the night going to end? Sickness upon men many times makes it impossible for them to rest, tossing about all night.

> Job 7:5 and 6:
> My flesh is clothed with worms and clods of dust; my skin is broken, and become loathsome. My days are swifter than a weaver's shuttle, and are spent without hope.

A weaver's shuttle was about the slowest machine. Job said, "That's what my captivity is today. My days are so slow, they move with the speed of a weaver's shuttle." This is an Orientalism used to show slowness. We might say, "Time moves as fast as molasses in January." When we have sickness upon our bodies, the days and nights inch by. When we have happiness, good health, and strength for good hard work, then the days pass speedily.

Job's second friend Bildad spoke in chapter eight.

Job 8:2:
How long wilt thou speak these *things?* and *how long shall* the words of thy mouth *be like* a strong wind?

"Your words are like a strong wind, Job. You are telling us you are a righteous man. You cannot kid us. We are your friends; we know you."

Job 8:6:
If thou *wert* pure and upright; surely now he would awake for thee, and make the habitation of thy righteousness prosperous.

Bildad looked at Job and said, "Job, you have a secret sin in your life; there is something wrong. You are out of alignment and harmony with God; therefore, this sickness is upon you. If you were pure and upright, God would let you prosper."

Job was beginning to come to the end of his
tolerance. He couldn't stand his friends' insinuations
much longer. He loved them, but they were making
life even more miserable for him, so he told them
so in chapter twelve.

> Job 12:2:
> No doubt but ye *are* the people, and wisdom
> shall die with you.

Job was being facetious with his friends. Job must
have had a good sense of humor. Being full of boils
and then having friends rub him the wrong way,
Job still quipped, "I suppose that when you three
fellows die (Professor Eliphaz, Rev. Bildad, and
Dr. Zophar) the world will be without wisdom."
So Job censured the arrogance and the pretentious-
ness of these friends. The Book of Job shows that
wicked men often prosper. Even the unjust who
practice the laws of God find that His laws work
for all who apply them. That the laws of God are
true and unchanging is the reason an unjust man
may prosper in the ways of the world, even as the
Book of Job clearly teaches. But, we must always
remember that God's judgments are not man's
judgments.

Job reproved his friends and continued to confess
his confidence in God. Not once throughout all the

chapters from four to forty does Job renounce
God or blame God for the evil which came upon him.
Job constantly kept confessing that God is righteous
and that He gives that which is good.

Job continued scolding his friends in chapter
thirteen.

Job 13:4:
But ye [my friends] *are* forgers of lies, ye
are all physicians of no value.

Job then makes his ultimate commitment.

Job 13:15:
Though he [God] slay me, yet will I trust in
him: but I will maintain mine own ways before
him.

In this verse the Orientalisms must be understood,
as they must be in many places in the Bible, because
the Bible is an Eastern book. The Bible uses Eastern
expressions of thought which are foreign to the
Western mind.* The Eastern man's expressions

*Two other scriptures in the Book of Job also necessitate this same
understanding of Orientalisms: Job 1:21 and 22: "...the Lord gave, and
the Lord hath taken away; blessed be the name of the Lord. In all this
Job sinned not, nor charged God foolishly." The word "foolishly" is
"with injustice." This is true because the Eastern man used these
expressions. Therefore, Job did not charge God with injustice, even
though the words were not spoken according to God's true actions.

attribute to God certain actions which, according to His Word, God is incapable of doing. The expressions are words from the lips of men, but the truths in the Bible clarify that God did not and would not do those things, as seen in Hebrews 2:14: "...through death he [Jesus Christ] might destroy him that had the power of death, that is, the devil." *God* is not going to slay Job; the power of death belongs to the Devil.

Job's statement of "though he slay me, yet will I trust in him" reminds us of the three men whom King Nebuchadnezzar threatened to have thrown into the fiery furnace. The Book of Daniel gives this account.

> Daniel 3:17 and 18:
> ...[The three believers say,] our God whom we serve is able to deliver us from the burning fiery furnace, and he will deliver *us* out of thine hand, O king.
> ...we will not serve thy gods...

That is believing; that is trust in God in the same proportions as Job's.

> Job 14:1 and 2:
> Man *that is* born of a woman *is* of few days, and full of trouble.

He cometh forth like a flower, and is cut down:
he fleeth also as a shadow, and continueth
not.

However, Job still retained his hope in the resurrection.

Job 14:14:
If a man die, shall he live *again?* all the days
of my appointed time will I wait, till my change
come.

In the fifteenth chapter, Eliphaz reproved Job for
justifying himself and accused him of being conceited.

Job 15:2, 11-13:
Should a wise man utter vain knowledge, and
fill his belly with the east wind?
Are the consolations of God small with thee?
is there any secret thing with thee?
Why doth thine heart carry thee away? and
what do thy eyes wink at,
That thou turnest thy spirit against God, and
lettest *such* words go out of thy mouth?

"Job, we cannot see it, but what are you overlooking? What is this evil you have in the background
of your mind? Try to justify yourself, but we know
you are full of sin. Come on, be honest."

Job rebuked his friends in his response to their harassments.

Job 16:2:
I have heard many such things: miserable comforters *are* ye all.

Job 19:2:
How long will ye vex my soul, and break me in pieces with words?

It is an easy thing to speak words that injure and harm while thinking you are doing good. Job said, "Your words break me in pieces."

Job 19:18 and 19:
Yea, young children despised me; I arose, and they spake against me.
All my inward friends abhorred me: and they whom I loved are turned against me.

Job said, "Now that I am sick, all the young children I used to talk to and take care of think that I am the one who is wrong. They think it is something I have done that has brought this sickness upon me, that it is my fault, and that I do not love God. All my friends have forsaken me."

Then Job gave a vivid description of his sickness.

Job 19:20:
My bone cleaveth to my skin and to my flesh, and I am escaped with the skin of my teeth.

In spite of his desperate condition, Job again stated his hope in a resurrection.

Job 19:25 and 26:
For I know *that* my redeemer liveth, and *that* he shall stand at the latter *day* upon the earth:
And *though* after my skin *worms* destroy this *body*, yet in my flesh shall I see God.

Even after suffering all his losses, his illnesses, and his miserable comforters, Job continued looking to God. Isn't that a wonderful confession to make, that the Lord is your redeemer, that you know your redeemer lives and that he will appear upon the earth and you shall see him?

In Sanskrit the last part of verse 26 is more accurately translated: "Although my body becomes frail and deteriorated, yet without my body shall I see God." According to God's Word, the resurrected ones will have a new body in the fashion of Christ's resurrected body. Therefore, "without my body" means without this present physical body which

57

corrupts, but in a new, resurrected body Job would see God.

In the twenty-first chapter, Job analyzed the prosperity of the wicked in detail. I want to take time at this point to clarify this important truth.

> Job 21:7-10:
> Wherefore do the wicked live, become old, yea, are mighty in power?
> Their seed is established in their sight with them, and their offspring before their eyes.
> Their houses *are* safe from fear, neither *is* the rod of God upon them.
> Their bull gendereth, and faileth not; their cow calveth, and casteth not her calf.

The reason the wicked man prospers, when a godly man seems not to, is due to the truth that the wicked man is not righteous in Christ, thus he belongs to the Devil. The Devil owns the unbeliever's life and everything he has. In contrast, the Devil has no legal rights over a man who has been born again of the Spirit of God, if that man will insist on the same. Therefore, the Devil will do his best to afflict, harm, and injure the Christian. There is no reason for the Devil to cast down the unbeliever who already belongs to him. The more Satan allows his own un-righteous ones to operate the immutable laws, which work for the just and the unjust alike, the more confused an unknowing Christian becomes. Satan will try to afflict the saint and let the sinner be blessed, reversing appearances so that the saint looks as the greatest sinner should.

In the twenty-second chapter of the Book of Job, Eliphaz again accused Job of many sins and asked him to repent.

Job 22:21-23:
Acquaint now thyself with him [God], and be at peace: thereby good shall come unto thee.
Receive, I pray thee, the law from his mouth, and lay up his words in thine heart.
If thou return to the Almighty, thou shalt be built up....

There could not have been truer words spoken, even if Jesus himself had spoken; but this accusation of having left or turned from the Almighty could not be placed against Job. The Bible says in the first chapter of this book that Job was a righteous man. If a sinner turns to God, he will get peace. When he puts God's words in his heart, the man will be edified.

I challenge you to start thinking about and believing this statement: Job 22:28: "Thou shalt also decree a thing, and it shall be established unto thee...." In other words, if you declare a promise of God, it must come to pass. What a great promise this is when we use it in our everyday living!

The story of Job moves on with Job's still maintaining that he is righteous, he has not wandered from God.

> Job 27:6 and 8:
> My righteousness I hold fast, and will not let it go: my heart shall not reproach *me* so long as I live.
> For what *is* the hope of the hypocrite, though he hath gained, when God taketh away his soul?

There is the whole key: holding fast our righteousness in our own minds. "God taketh away his soul" is again the Orientalism, an Eastern expression, not truth. God doesn't take away the soul because that is in the Devil's power.

Finally, Job's three friends tired of talking to Job because Job confessed his righteousness in God. His three friends couldn't understand it.

Job 32:1:
So these three men ceased to answer Job, because he *was* righteous in his own eyes.

There then appeared a new man on the scene. This man, Elihu, was angry with Job and also with Job's three friends.

Job 32:2 and 3:
Then was kindled the wrath of Elihu the son of Barachel the Buzite...against Job was his wrath kindled, because he justified himself rather than God.
Also against his three friends was his [Elihu's] wrath kindled, because they had found no answer, and *yet* had condemned Job.

Well, Elihu was not smarter, I assure you, than those with whom he was angry. He was very unkind to Job throughout the conversation.

As we read various scattered verses from Job, I just want to call to your attention a very beautiful verse.

Job 35:10:
...Where *is* God my maker, who giveth songs in the night.

It's a wonderful thing to know that you and God are right. God's spirit within you has made you righteous; so, no matter what your friends say, you know that you have a "song in the night."

God spoke to Job in chapter thirty-eight.

> Job 38:22 and 23:
> Hast thou [Job] entered into the treasures of the snow? or hast thou seen the treasures of the hail,
> Which I have reserved against the time of trouble, against the day of battle and war?

Are there treasures in snow and hail? The twenty-third verse is still future. Scientists came up a few years ago with a bold declaration that there are "floating ice cubes" weighing two and three hundred pounds each floating in space. I do not know if they are right or wrong, but my Bible says that there are going to be great hail stones, "...the treasures of the hail, which I have reserved against the time of trouble...." We simply thrill with the revelation of those men many, many thousands of years ago.

> Job 38:31:
> Canst thou bind the sweet influences of Pleiades, or loose the bands of Orion?

This was written in Job thousands of years before the coming of Jesus. Man talked about the Pleiades and the bands of Orion, yet our astronomers have not known anything about them for more than perhaps a few hundred years.

Job 38:32:
...canst thou guide Arcturus with his sons?

Arcturus is another one of the stars. Arcturus is always on time, never off a second. "Job, can you guide Arcturus or does God guide it?"

Job 40:2-5:
Shall he that contendeth with the Almighty instruct *him?* he that reproveth God, let him answer it.
Then Job answered the Lord, and said, Behold, I am vile; what shall I answer thee? I will lay mine hand upon my mouth.
Once have I spoken; but I will not answer: yea, twice; but I will proceed no further.

In other words, even though a man is righteous before God, he does not go around bragging about his righteousness to men upon earth. Do not brag about your righteousness, but claim your righteousness, live it. Do not boast that you are righteous because,

63

are you the fellow that keeps Arcturus in its course? Job said, "I am vile...."

God spoke to Job again in the last part of the fortieth chapter about His power, finally concluding His message to Job at the end of the forty-first chapter. In Job 42, Job responded.

> Job 42:1-5:
> Then Job answered the Lord, and said,
> I know that thou canst do every *thing*, and *that* no thought can be withholden from thee.
> Who *is* he that hideth counsel without knowledge? therefore have I uttered that I understood not; things too wonderful for me, which I knew not.
> Hear, I beseech thee, and I will speak: I will demand of thee, and declare thou unto me.
> I have heard of thee by the hearing of the ear: but now mine eye seeth thee.

There is a tremendous difference between hearing about God and seeing God for oneself. Job said, "Up until this time, while I had all this abundance upon my life, I only heard of thee with the hearing of the ear. But since I have come through this, I now see." It is wonderful that a man may be a Christian today and come through a period of affliction or a period of sickness which Satan brings upon him, and all at once his believing rises and he has power to overcome his circumstances. That man taps the resources by positive believing and God delivers him from Satan's captivity. Many of us have mainly heard of God by the hearing of the ears. But we grow spiritually as we believe the Word of God. We see that God lives and moves and has His being in people today, and we discover He is the same today as He was yesterday or will be tomorrow. This is the day to believe to see.

Job said, "Up until this time I have just heard about you, God, but now I see." What did he hear? Oh, he heard that God was peaceful and kind; God was considerate; he heard that God heals people. "But now I see."

Then God made a promise to Job, Job acted upon the promise, and God fulfilled it. This is the principle to apply in our lives when we want our prayers answered.

Job's Deliverance

Job admitted in Job 42:5 that "I have heard of thee by the hearing of the ear: but now my eye seeth thee." Once Job "saw God," God was able to do a most wonderful thing for Job—He delivered him. But in the sequence of events, God first corrected Job's three friends.

Job 42:7:
And it was *so*, that after the Lord had spoken these words unto Job, the Lord said to Eliphaz the Temanite, My wrath is kindled against thee, and against thy two friends: for ye have not spoken of me *the thing that is* right, as my servant Job *hath*.

The Lord was angry with Job's three friends, his "miserable comforters." Originally, these men had come to pray for Job; but, instead, God commanded that Job pray for them.

Job 42:8 and 9:
Therefore take unto you [God was still speaking to Eliphaz] now seven bullocks and seven rams, and go to my servant Job, and offer up for yourselves a burnt offering; and my servant Job shall pray for you: for him will I accept: lest I deal with you *after your* folly, in that ye have not spoken of me *the thing which is* right, like my servant Job.
So Eliphaz the Temanite and Bildad the Shuhite *and* Zophar the Naamathite went, and did according as the Lord commanded them: the Lord also accepted Job.

Then comes this powerful, succinct verse that tells of God's fulfillment of His Word.

Job 42:10:
And the Lord turned the captivity of Job, when he prayed for his friends: also the Lord gave Job twice as much as he had before.

Satan brought the captivity, but the Lord reversed it by freeing Job. In one short verse of scripture we learn two great truths: God delivered Job from Satan's captivity and then gave to Job double what he previously had when he already had been the wealthiest man in the East. The Word says, "...the Lord turned the captivity of Job...." Satan would

68

never have reversed it. When did God reverse his captivity? When Job prayed for his friends.

There is a wonderful key. I have found that sometimes when people start ministering to others, they receive their own healing. As Job prayed for his friends, he received blessings for himself also.

As Job obeyed the Word of God and prayed for his friends, God turned the captivity of Job. God also did something more: "...also the Lord gave Job twice as much as he had before." Job 42 gives the specifics.

> Job 42:12 and 13:
> So the Lord blessed the latter end of Job more than his beginning: for he had fourteen thousand sheep, and six thousand camels, and a thousand yoke of oxen, and a thousand she asses.
> He had also seven sons and three daughters.

During the 140 years that Job lived after his deliverance, God added to Job's substance until he possessed double his original possessions, with the exception of his children.

> Job 42:16 and 17:
> After this lived Job an hundred and forty years, and saw his sons, and his sons' sons,

even four generations.
So Job died, *being* old and full of days.

Isn't that wonderful! A man of God walking through life may have a temporary captivity, but the Lord can break the chains of bondage and set him free. Job had a full life.

Do you think that when a person dies at the age of twenty in an automobile accident he has had a full life? Who is aborting our lives when we have heart trouble and die between thirty and forty years of age? Who has the power of death? Hebrews 2:14 contains the answer.

Hebrews 2:14:
Forasmuch then as the children are partakers of flesh and blood, he also himself likewise took part of the same; that through death he might destroy him that had the power of death, that is, the devil.

If we give him opportunity, Satan will capture and ruin us. Yet, the Devil has no legal rights over a believer. You and I must claim our God-given protection and abundance.

I want to close by showing one more important point. Sometimes we as children of God do not claim our deliverance from the tricks of Satan. At these times Satan may overcome us in our minds and flesh, but he cannot touch the spirit from God in us. Satan cannot destroy the spirit which came when we were born again, for the nature of God in us is *eternal life*. This spirit, which is the anointing of God, cannot be taken away and cannot die. God just cannot be defeated by Satan in any way. Christians, believe God and be delivered from every captivity now! Let it be said of you, as it was of Job, "And the Lord turned the captivity." Don't just hear of God's power with your ears; see it with your eyes by receiving God's abundant goodness.

Part II

A Believer's Walk

Part II

A Believer's Walk

To adequately discuss a believer's walk would take us verse by verse through God's entire Word. So the following chapters are simply a light touch on points relating to this broad topic. Although this is not a comprehensive study of the walk of believer's the four studies trace many points which are very profitable ones to keep in mind and to cultivate.

The first key in "A Believer's Walk" is that of commitment. Dedicated commitment is a Biblical principle in practice where commitment is the primary step to acting and thereby gaining results. As children of God we must become fully persuaded of, totally committed to, the ministry of reconciliation of Jesus Christ and then have the energy to carry through on that conviction and reap the harvest of men.

"The Joy of Our Hearts" explains that joy is indeed *not* synonymous with happiness, for happiness is a product of pleasing circumstances or events, whereas joy is an internal quality. God gave us joy when we were born again. And as we walk in fellowship with Him according to His Word, our joy overflows; it comes into manifestation in our lives.

To further help us believers in our Christian walks, God not only gave us His Word, but He also gave us people, as examples, to imitate. This concept was established when Paul wrote that the Thessalonians had become followers, or imitators, of him when he had disclosed to them the gospel both in word and in power. They chose to imitate Paul's example. God gives us men and women of God who are responsible to lead us, as examples, in their practice of truth.

In observing and imitating examples, Abraham should be a primary focal point. Abraham took God at His word. God's Word says that Abraham staggered not at God's promise; and, because of this, God made Abraham "the father of all them that believe." What a joy this promise must have been to Abraham. What a joy it is to us to have his example of commitment.

A believer's walk is a learning situation. And God has made available such helpful knowledge and assistance that we may mature in the family of God and become more and more like the Lord Jesus Christ.

CHAPTER FOUR

The Energy of Your Conviction

In September of 1935, a Californian by the name of Tilly Lewis opened a tomato canning factory which her advisers had warned her would never get off the ground. They had two reasons for their doubt: (1) agriculturalists thought that Italian tomatoes would not grow successfully in California and (2) the manager, being a woman, could never acquire the financial backing needed to open a major canning operation. Despite other's pessimism, in that year Tilly Lewis got the money, and her factory was in full operation, cooking for the first time beautiful California-grown Italian tomatoes. Her idea had taken concrete form, and now she would be able to prove what she had known all along.

But early in the processing plant's operation—at a very critical moment—the new steam boilers which were cooking the ripe tomatoes broke down. Something mechanical had gone wrong. The steam was going down. For a moment Tilly was frantic. Here she

75

had spent many dedicated years getting ready for this event and then, beyond her control, her dream seemed to be shattering. After her initial panic, Tilly told all the workers to remain at their posts, that she would be back. She then went for a walk by herself out into an open area where she sat down and got quiet. After sitting a few minutes, Tilly faintly detected a locomotive whistle in the wind. She ran back to the building, got on a telephone and called the locomotive offices in that area of California. Within two hours, arrangements had been made and a locomotive engine was sitting on a side track pumping steam into the boilers, and the tomatoes began cooking again. In 1973, according to the record, this corporation begun by Tilly Lewis did forty million dollars' worth of business. Tilly Lewis had had the energy to carry through on her conviction. In other words, she had the perseverance to stick with her idea or plan and she has been rewarded abundantly for it.

According to his biographers, Thomas Edison was a completely apathetic student. What then made him America's most versatile and successful inventor? The energy of his conviction. He became stimulated by ideas and possibilities, and he worked on them until he reached a conclusion to his ideas.

Albert Einstein was also a backward student with very little formal education. What made him such an intellectual explosion? Henry Ford had only a few years in a one-room public school. What made him a success? Al Smith was a four-term governor of the state of New York who also ran for the presidency of the United States, yet he never went beyond the seventh grade. Ezra Cornell, founder of Cornell University and also the organizer and originator of the Western Union Telegraph Company, never graduated from any school whatsoever. George Bernard Shaw, one of the world's great modern writers, only went through the fifth grade. Did you know that Grandma Moses never took one lesson in painting?

We know that every effect has a cause, so there has to be an explanation why these people became outstandingly successful. George Fox, the founder of the Quaker sect, admitted that he was inferior to others in every personal aspect except for one: the energy to carry through on his conviction. He was fully persuaded of the endeavor which he pursued. As I have looked at the lives of people, I have seen that it has always been the energy to back up and carry out their convictions that has made their lives successful and outstanding.

If success had depended upon formal education, then there is no explanation for an Edison, an Einstein, a Henry Ford, an Al Smith, an Ezra Cornell, a George Bernard Shaw, a Grandma Moses or many others. But their successes did not stem from just

77

knowledge or raw ability. Their achievements were
the result of steadfastly applying principles that can
be found in God's Word. In short, they believed to
the extent of acting on their beliefs. And, furthermore, they not only acted, they persevered with
their various endeavors.

There is a record in Romans which will set some
of these great truths in our lives from God's Word by
giving us the example of Abraham.

> Romans 4:18-21:
> Who [Abraham] against hope believed in hope,
> that he might become the father of many
> nations; according to that which was spoken,
> So shall thy seed be.
> And being not weak in faith [believing], he
> considered not his own body now dead, when
> he was about an hundred years old [he was 99],
> neither yet the deadness of Sara's womb [she
> was 90]:
> He staggered not at the promise of God through
> unbelief; but was strong in faith [believing],
> giving glory to God;
> And being fully persuaded that, what he [God]
> had promised, he [God] was able also to perform.

There is the reason for the success of Abraham.
He was fully persuaded. Abraham held fast to God's

Word—he "staggered not at the promise of God through unbelief." Even though it had not come to pass by the time Abraham was 99 and Sara 90, he did not lose his confidence in God's Word. He was absolutely sure that God would carry out His promise. That unwavering certainty is what brought about the greatness of Abraham to the end that he is credited as the father of all those who believe. What a tremendous credit to receive.

The great things of this world are available to men and women who know how to operate one of God's laws, namely the law of "believing equals receiving." And this law includes "believing equals action." Great accomplishments are not necessarily just for people with great intellectual ability; they are attainable by men and women who believe to receive. It doesn't hurt to have a few brains, but it doesn't help unless one operates this universal law of believing. Many operate the law of believing without even having a knowledge of God's Word, for this law of believing works for saint and sinner alike. But for those who haven't been operating and therefore benefiting from the law of positive believing, a knowledge of it from God's Word can open the door to change course and set sail on the new, better way.

Like Abraham, Jesus Christ must also have been fully persuaded. To cite one example, the fourth chapter of the Gospel of John gives an account of the disciples becoming very concerned about their master because he wasn't eating when they thought he should be hungry.

> John 4:31-34:
> In the mean while his disciples prayed him, saying, Master, eat.
> But he said unto them, I have meat to eat that ye know not of.
> Therefore said the disciples one to another, Hath any man brought him *ought* to eat?
> Jesus saith unto them, My meat is to do the will of him that sent me, and to finish his work.

God had sent Jesus Christ and he was to do God's work. Now to do God's work, with singleness of mind, Jesus must have been fully persuaded. The account of Jesus in John 4 continues.

> Verse 35:
> Say not ye, There are yet four months, and *then* cometh harvest? behold, I say unto you, Lift up your eyes, and look on the fields; for they are white already to harvest.

This pointedly demonstrates the difference in people. Some people see the outreach of God's Word sometime in the future. *We* must see it in the immediate present. Followers said to Jesus, "Four months yet till harvest." But Jesus knew that the important "crop" was ripe at that very moment. The disciples didn't perceive this because they were not yet fully persuaded. They had not begun generating energy for their conviction. They were not utterly convinced and committed to their cause. They were still mentally assenting but not acting on their conviction.

"Lift up your eyes," Jesus Christ said. That's the message to the Church of the Body today. Get your eyes up. Don't look at the things of the world with all of its confusion and negatives. These will limit you. Look at God and the things of God. Get your vision elevated and then carry through on your conviction. The rationalists will say, "Four months till harvest." God says, "Now is the time; today is the day of salvation. Open up your spiritual eyes." Get your vision up to where God is magnetically drawing you with the Lord Jesus Christ in all his glory and power. "For the fields are white already to harvest."

Now, you've got to get fully persuaded that you are what the Word of God says you are and that you have what the Word of God says you have. Then you can do what the Word of God says you can do. You must be convinced *before* you can accomplish your goals.

You and I have only one responsibility to God and that is to live for Him with all the energy and ability that we have. As sons we are to walk fully persuaded in what He has made us. If God redeemed us, if God saved and filled us, and if God gave us everything He says He gave us in the Word, the least we can do is to commit ourselves fully to Him. Then He will supply each and every need.

> Matthew 6:34:
> Take therefore no thought [have no anxiety] for the morrow: for the morrow shall take thought for the things of itself. Sufficient unto the day *is* the evil thereof.

In other words, don't get anxious about tomorrow. You just walk with the greatness of that full commitment today, and tomorrow will take care of itself when it comes. We can only live now. This is the moment. The past moment you can't relive. The one still coming you can't live yet. You are living one moment at a time. When we begin to become fully persuaded moment by moment, we'll make it through each day living the more abundant life.

Someone once said, "I think and I think and I think, and all I ever get is a pain in my thinker." You can get like that about God and His Word. You think you have a theological system all worked out except that it seemingly doesn't work. You can rationalize God's Word into fruitlessness. The greatness of God in our lives is brought to pass not by our intelligence, but in our commitment—being fully persuaded and belonging to Him. Thus, the primary ingredient is belief. Each individual will go as far as his believing takes him. A great example was the Apostle Paul.

> II Timothy 1:11 and 12:
> ...I am appointed a preacher, and an apostle, and a teacher of the Gentiles.
> For the which cause [the cause of the gospel of the grace of God] I also suffer these things: nevertheless I am not ashamed: for I know whom I have believed, and am persuaded that he is able to keep that which I have committed unto him against that day.

This literally should read: "I know whom I have believed, and am persuaded [fully persuaded beyond a shadow of a doubt] that He [God] is able to keep my deposit which He has committed [given] unto me against [until] that day." This accurate translation is given in the margins of the 1881 and 1901 Revised Versions. What a tremendous record from God's Word. To be fully persuaded is to know that even if you were in the midst of hell itself, God will keep that deposit which He gave to you. And that deposit is the revelation of the mystery, that it is Christ in you, the hope of glory.

Paul was fully persuaded and, consequently, fully committed. That is why his ministry lives in the epistles. That is also the reason God's work is carried out today. Because men and women like us are fully persuaded and have the assurance that God will keep that which He has promised. Being fully convinced, Paul was able to carry through and convince others of the saving grace and power of Christ Jesus. That is why you too should become fully persuaded of the integrity and accuracy of the revelation addressed to the Church of the Body. Become fully persuaded, then you will have energy to carry out your conviction and reap the harvest that is ripe.

CHAPTER FIVE

The Joy of Our Hearts

Recently four people came to me individually on the same day, and unknowingly, wanted to discuss the same subject. All of them related their experiences of having so much joy in their lives since the Word of God had been taught to them and since they began living that Word. The joy of the Word had made their lives so exciting that they bubbled from one day to the next. If a perplexing situation did indeed come up, they would face it with God's Word, go to bed that night and say, "Well, Lord, I thank you that this day is finished. Hallelujah! Amen!" And immediately they would go to sleep. The next morning these people would wake up with great anticipation of the new day, having the joy of knowing that God's blessing was upon their families and their work. The people lived their lives with joy.

God's Word tells of various types of joy. Joy is a very important quality which God wants us to have.

85

So it is this one word "joy" we want to investigate that we can know the fullness of our joy. Let us begin our study with the great revelation of Jesus' joy told in Hebrews 12.

> Hebrews 12:1 and 2:
> Wherefore seeing we also are compassed about with so great a cloud of witnesses, let us lay aside every weight, and the sin which doth so easily beset *us,* and let us run with patience the race that is set before us,
> Looking unto Jesus the author and finisher of *our* faith; who for the joy that was set before him endured the cross, despising the shame, and is set down at the right hand of the throne of God.

We are surrounded by a great cloud of witnesses, referring to all those believers mentioned in the previous chapter of Hebrews and including everyone who knows and believes God's Word. They are our examples. By the testimony of their believing we can do the same wonderful works they did as we walk for God. Because we are encircled by such examples, "let us lay aside every weight, and the sin which doth so easily beset *us.*" *We* have to lay aside the weight and the sin. Our own action determines the casting off of the entanglements of this world. God didn't tell us to pray about laying them aside; He said, "Do it."

"Let us run with patience the race that is set before us." In order to meet the challenge of the race, we must be disciplined and in condition from practicing.

> Hebrews 12:2a:
> Looking unto Jesus [who is] the author and finisher of *our* faith *[pistis]*....

We run this race by focusing solely on one person, the Lord Jesus Christ. He is the author, the starter, and also the finisher of faith. What a witness. What an example for us to follow.

> Verse 2b:
> ...who for the joy that was set before him endured the cross, despising the shame, and is set down at the right hand of the throne of God.

Was the cross a joy? No. But Jesus Christ saw beyond the cross—beyond the punishment, the crown of thorns, the spitting in the face, the whipping. "For the joy that was set before him," because of the anticipation of the future, Jesus was able to endure the cross, "despising the shame, and is set down at the right hand of the throne of God." What a contrast to go from a shameful cross to the right hand of the throne of God.

Jesus Christ felt within himself this quality of joy. Joy is an inside quality. Happiness depends on the things with which we are surrounded, while joy is never dependent upon our surroundings.* Joy is something that comes from within. Just as a rock remains steady no matter how the waves slap or the winds blow, we still have joy because we know where we are going, even in the midst of the most trying circumstances. We know the outcome because we are assured of seeing Him face to face. We can walk with an abundance of joy because joy is a quality lodging deep within us. Joy is not dependent upon the environment or the circumstances in which we may or may not be engulfed. It is dependent upon what Jesus Christ wrought for us.

> Psalms 16:8:
> I have set the Lord always before me: because *he is* at my right hand, I shall not be moved.

If and when we have come to the place where we put God first *always*, then we shall not be moved. Putting God first, being so absolutely sure that what God said He meant and that His Word is His will, we are unmovable. No one is steadfast at all times and in all points. But as we grow in the knowledge and the grace of the greatness of God's Word, we be-

*The Greek word for "joy," *chara*, comes from *chairo*, from which is also derived *charisma*, gift from God.

come more certain; and the more we believe, the more sure we become, the greater the joy we have in living. This same sixteenth psalm which says God is at my right hand, three verses later gives us more edification.

Psalms 16:11:
Thou wilt shew me the path of life: in thy presence *is* fulness of joy; at thy right hand *there are* pleasures for evermore.

"Thou wilt shew me the path of life: in thy [God's] presence *is* fulness of joy...." Not just half joy, not just 99 percent joy, but full joy comes in God's presence. If we want this fullness of joy, we have to get into that presence of God in Christ where "*there are* pleasures for evermore."

Psalms 105 speaks of God and the children of Israel and tells that the Egyptians were glad when Israel left Egypt.

Psalms 105:37 and 38:
He [God] brought them [the children of Israel] forth [out of Egypt] also with silver and gold: and *there was* not one feeble *person* among their tribes.
Egypt was glad when they departed: for the fear of them [the children of Israel] fell upon them [the Egyptians].

Our enemies will become perplexed by us too when we have this unmovable joy deep within. We can become so full of joy that our foes won't be able to understand what is going on. They will be like the Egyptians who were glad when the children of Israel departed.

> Psalms 105:39-42:
> He [God] spread a cloud for a covering; and fire to give light in the night.
> *The people* asked, and he [God] brought quails, and satisfied them with the bread of heaven.
> He opened the rock, and the waters gushed out; they ran in the dry places *like* a river.
> For he [God] remembered his holy promise, *and* Abraham his servant.

God remembered His holy promise to Abraham His servant, and God brought forth His people. Then will God not remember us? Will He not remember His promises to the Body of Christ, the Church, His sons?

> Psalms 105:43:
> And he brought forth his people with joy, *and* his chosen with gladness.

For God to deliver His people is a joy to Him. You never knew God had joy? He surely does. When He brought Israel out of Egypt, "...he brought forth his people with joy...." It was a joy to God to deliver His people. He brought them out of Egypt with possessions of silver and gold. There wasn't one feeble person among them. God led them with a cloud by day and a pillar of fire by night. He gave them food to eat and water to drink. They had all their needs met. God was pleased that He had the privilege of doing all these things for Israel.

God also has joy today when He delivers people. It brings joy to the heart of God that He has people who come to Him and say, "I need a little help, Father. I thank you for giving it to me according to the promise of Your Word and for remembering the promises that You made to us as Your sons."

> Psalms 105:43-45:
> And he brought forth his people with joy, *and* his chosen with gladness:
> And gave them the lands of the heathen: and they inherited the labour of the people;
> That they might observe his statutes, and keep his laws. Praise ye the Lord.

Isn't that beautiful! God is full of joy to help His children who in turn carry out His Word.

Jeremiah 36:23 relates the experience of an angry king who took his penknife and cut up one of the scrolls of the Holy Scriptures, God's Word. Showing no regard for God, the king tossed the pieces into the fireplace. An earlier account in Jeremiah tells that when God's people returned from many years of captivity, another scroll was found beneath the debris which had accumulated in the temple area. In contrast to the angry king, Jeremiah's feelings and action in finding a copy of God's Word were very different.

> Jeremiah 15:16:
> Thy words were found, and I did eat them; and thy word was unto me the joy and rejoicing of mine heart: for I am called by thy name, O Lord God of hosts.

God's Word was unto Jeremiah joy and rejoicing. Not just joy, but joy and "re-joy" over and over again. Rejoicing is a repeated performance of joy.

Isn't this true for so many of us? The first time we really ate the sweetness of God's Word, it was a tremendous joy. We savored it, and we still like to savor that Word over and over again. Every time we hear God's Word, we rejoice in it. That is why the Word *is* joy. In God's presence there is joy. God's joy is the deliverance of His people and it is His Word that is the joy of the believer.

92

I Thessalonians 1:2-6:

We give thanks to God always for you all, making mention of you in our prayers;

Remembering without ceasing your work of faith [believing], and [your] labour of love, and patience of hope in our Lord Jesus Christ, in the sight of God and our Father;

Knowing, brethren beloved, your election of God.

For our gospel came not unto you in word only, but also in power, and in the Holy Ghost, and in much assurance; as ye know what manner of men we were among you for your sake.

And ye became followers of us, and of the Lord, having received the word in much affliction, with joy of the Holy Ghost *[pneuma hagion]*.

What a tremendous truth to receive the Word with joy as Jeremiah did when he found the Word and as the believers did in Thessalonica in the first century. Did they have a few afflictions? Were they surrounded with unbelief, persecution, paganism, idolatry? Certainly, but that didn't make any difference. Even if we are right in the midst of all negatives, we can have joy because joy is an inner quality. It comes by renewing our minds on the Word and letting the presence of that Word stay there, absolutely refusing to allow anybody or anything to interfere with it.

The Book of Acts contains a record that teaches us some of the great, great truths on joy.

> Acts 8:4-8:
> Therefore they [the believers from Jerusalem] that were scattered abroad went every where preaching the word.
> Then Philip went down to the city of Samaria, and preached Christ unto them.
> And the people with one accord gave heed unto those things which Philip spake, hearing and seeing the miracles which he did.
> For unclean spirits, crying with loud voice, came out of many that were possessed *with them:* and many taken with palsies, and that were lame, were healed.
> And there was great joy in that city.

The believers from Jerusalem were scattered abroad because of persecution. Yet, because they were scattered, they spread God's Word in many new places. And they went everywhere preaching the very same thing that brought on the persecution in the first place. As at least one believer, Philip, spoke the Word and it began to gain preeminence in Samaria, many people were released from their afflictions. And there was great joy in Samaria because of the way the Word of God moved in that community. There was great joy in that city because the Word had permeated the lives of people, and they saw signs, miracles, and wonders. This is always a great joy. Is there any greater joy than when one of us leads someone into the new birth or when we lead someone into the manifestation of the holy spirit or when we share just one little word or one verse which really helps a person? Is there joy in seeing someone delivered from bondage by healing or a miracle? Could we buy that at any price? That is joy; that is an inside benefit. What a tremendous blessing joy is.

In Luke 15 we learn of the joy felt even in heaven when one person turns to the true God and His Word.

> Luke 15:7:
> I say unto you, that likewise joy shall be in heaven over one sinner that repenteth, more than over ninety and nine just persons, which need no repentance.

Every time someone turns to the true God and His Word even the angels in heaven are joyful. All heaven resounds with joy when a person is born again of God's Spirit. All the angels of God are joyful, and God Himself is so full of joy that He will do anything for any person according to His Word when that individual believes.

This verse in Luke 15 does not indicate that God doesn't love those who are already in His family.

It is expressing and focusing on the exciting joy He feels when He welcomes a new son. This is the thrill of having a new baby. The older children are certainly loved, but great joy is brought about by the coming of a new baby.

When we study this word "joy" throughout the Word of God, we find that in God's presence there is much joy.

> I John 1:4:
> And these things write we unto you, that your joy may be full.

The things written in the Word of God are written that our joy may be full. God gave us joy when we were born again. Now, as we walk in fellowship with Him according to the Word, our joy overflows, it comes into fruition in our lives. The revealed or written Word is joy to people as they receive it. When Philip was in Samaria, the whole city was filled with joy. The angels in heaven have joy over salvation. And now we read that the Word is written not to frustrate people, not to defeat them, not to enslave them, but to fill them with joy.

And then we have the truth about another source of joy in Galatians 5:22.

> But the fruit of the Spirit is love, joy....

One element of the fruit of the spirit is joy. New fruit is brought about as we operate the manifestations of the spirit. As we cultivate by the process of the operation of the manifestations, we produce the fruit of the spirit—one of which is joy. So we cultivate and we produce fruit. Operate the manifestations of the spirit—speaking in tongues, interpretation of tongues, prophecy, word of knowledge, word of wisdom, discerning of spirits, faith, miracles and healing—and joy will definitely be produced. God's Word says so.

In Philippians we learn that the Apostle Paul experienced joy for his brethren.

> Philippians 4:1:
> Therefore, my brethren dearly beloved and longed for, my joy and crown, so stand fast in the Lord, *my* dearly beloved.

There is joy when we help bring people to a knowledge of God's Word, when we bring them unto salvation and into the fullness of the spirit. Paul said to the Philippians that they were his joy because he had led them to the Lord and he had taught them the Word. As these people walked on the Word, they were his joy. Whenever we nurture someone up in the Lord, we realize this same joy.

97

We began this short study of the joy of our hearts in seeing that Jesus "...for the joy that was set before him endured the cross." I am sure that the Apostle Paul was not always pleased with his experiences; but what gave him joy was seeing growth and steadfastness in the people he had taught and the anticipation of Christ's return. Paul declared in Acts 20:24 "...that I might finish my course with joy...." In the midst of the greatest problems with which we could be surrounded, there is still the opportunity for us to overflow with joy deep within. We also ought to have joy that we are in a race. We should keep running with joy the full course of that ministry which we have received. As we read in Hebrews 2, we should never slack off on the ministry.

> Hebrews 2:1:
> Therefore we ought to give the more earnest heed to the things which we have heard, lest at any time we should let *them* slip.

We should pay "the more earnest heed to the things which we have heard," namely, the accuracy of God's Word, "lest at any time we should let *them* slip." All of us in this ministry have an abundance of joy today compared with what we had before we heard God's Word and the knowledge of how to live according to its teaching. Therefore, we should be absolutely "stedfast, unmoveable, always abounding in the work of the Lord," as I Corinthians 15:58 says, giving the more earnest heed to that Word and steadfastly applying it.

> Hebrews 2:2-4:
> For if the word spoken by angels was stedfast, and every transgression and disobedience received a just recompence of reward;
> How shall we escape, if we neglect so great salvation; which at the first began to be spoken by the Lord, and was confirmed unto us by them that heard *him;*
> God also bearing *them* witness, both with signs and wonders, and with divers miracles, and gifts of the Holy Ghost, according to his own will?

We should always be steadfast on God's Word for it is that Word and the accuracy of it that makes possible our joy and rejoicing. What a wonderful opportunity and privilege it is to have joy in the kind of world in which we live. Generally, the people we meet just don't have it. For us to have this joy is a beautiful example of what God is not only able, but willing to do for us His children. Wherever we go and whatever we do, we have that joy within.

To manifest the joy within we must manifest the love of God in the renewed mind. We do not hesitate to speak God's Word, but we share it lovingly with great joy. Then the people who receive it will also have great joy. Therefore, the angels will rejoice; God will rejoice; we will rejoice.

Those of us who are born again of God's Spirit are lights shining in the darkness. We have to hold forth God's light, which is His Word. We have to manifest the greatness of the love of God which is in Christ Jesus. That is our joy.

So don't be discouraged or downcast. Don't let people deceive you with the things which bring superficial happiness. Just know that we have God's joy on the inside. And we can manifest more and more of that abundant joy daily as we walk on the accuracy of God's Word.

Followers of Us

The Apostle Paul's first epistle to the Thessalonians tells a dynamic story. The church at Thessalonica was a living, faithful church, one who stood by Paul and labored lovingly as they waited hopefully for the return of Christ. Because the Thessalonian church believed God's Word as it was taught to them by Paul and remained faithful to it, this church became an example to other churches in that region of Asia Minor. What did the believers in Thessalonica do to become an example for others to model themselves after? The founding of the Thessalonian church is told in Acts 17.

Acts 17:1 and 2:
Now when they [Paul and Silas] had passed through Amphipolis and Apollonia, they came to Thessalonica, where was a synagogue of the Jews:
And Paul, as his manner was, went in unto

them, and three sabbath days reasoned with
them out of the scriptures.

Paul's manner gave his listeners time to consider
his words for he spent three Sabbaths in the synagogue reasoning with them from the Scriptures.

Acts 17:3-6:
Opening and alleging, that Christ must needs
have suffered, and risen again from the dead;
and that this Jesus, whom I preach unto you,
is Christ.
And some of them believed, and consorted
with Paul and Silas; and of the devout Greeks
a great multitude, and of the chief women not a
few.
But the Jews which believed not, moved with
envy, took unto them certain lewd fellows of
the baser sort, and gathered a company, and set
all the city on an uproar, and assaulted the
house of Jason, and sought to bring them out to
the people.
And when they found them not, they drew
Jason and certain brethren unto the rulers of
the city, crying, These that have turned the
world upside down are come hither also.

This scripture about turning the world upside
down is one I always have in my mind when I talk

about God's Word turning the world right side up. The world was already upside down and topsy-turvy when Paul came with the greatness of God's Word to Thessalonica. He turned it upside down, which simply means he got it right side up as it ought to have been.

Acts 17:7-11:
[Paul and Silas] Whom Jason hath received: and these all do contrary to the decrees of Caesar, saying that there is another king, *one* Jesus.

And they troubled the people and the rulers of the city, when they heard these things.

And when they had taken security of Jason, and of the other, they let them go.

And the brethren immediately sent away Paul and Silas by night unto Berea: who coming *thither* went into the synagogue of the Jews.

These were more noble than those in Thessalonica, in that they received the word with all readiness of mind, and searched the scriptures daily, whether those things were so.

When men of God such as Paul and Silas ran into trouble with people who were not appreciating God's Word, they simply moved on to another area, always looking for people who would receive the Word of

God with all readiness of mind and study the Word to make sure they were being taught God's truth.

> Acts 17:12-15:
> Therefore many of them [of Berea] believed; also of honourable women which were Greeks, and of men, not a few.
> But when the Jews of Thessalonica had knowledge that the word of God was preached of Paul at Berea, they came thither also, and stirred up the people.
> And then immediately the brethren sent away Paul to go as it were to the sea: but Silas and Timotheus abode there still.
> And they that conducted Paul brought him unto Athens: and receiving a commandment unto Silas and Timotheus for to come to him with all speed, they departed.

With all the havoc that the Jews at Thessalonica were stirring up, it shows how steadfast and convinced the believers in that place had to have been. When we understand these circumstances and activities of the unbelievers in Thessalonica, we can more fully appreciate the context in which Paul wrote to the church there. Look now at the beginning of the letter to the church at Thessalonica.

I Thessalonians 1:1:
Paul, and Silvanus [Silas], and Timotheus,
unto the church of the Thessalonians *which is*
in God the Father and *in* the Lord Jesus Christ:
Grace *be* unto you, and peace, from God our
Father, and the Lord Jesus Christ.

This salutation in itself is filled with wonderful
truths. The word "in" after "Thessalonians" is the
Greek word *en,* which here should be translated
"by." The only way you ever have a church in
Thessalonica or any other place is *by* God the Father,
by what God does in the lives of people. The Church
then and now is by God the Father because we are
His sons. We are also by the Lord Jesus Christ because
it is by believing on the Lord Jesus Christ—confessing
with our mouth Jesus as lord and believing that
God raised him from the dead—that we are born
again.* What a tremendous greeting to the church
of Thessalonica.

The salutation continues, "...Grace *be* unto you,
and peace, from God our Father, and the Lord Jesus
Christ." The first thing Paul tells the church is that it

---

*Romans 10:9 and 10: "That if thou shalt confess with thy mouth the
Lord Jesus, and shalt believe in thine heart that God hath raised him
from the dead, thou shalt be saved. For with the heart man believeth
unto righteousness; and with the mouth confession is made unto
salvation."

is an age of grace—not good works, but grace. The grace, divine favor, *charis*, is what gives us the peace spoken of in I Thessalonians 1:1. People who try to work for salvation are never peaceful; they are miserable. There is nothing more wonderful than to have God's grace and be at peace within yourself: you're not disturbed on the inside; you just know that you know that you know that you are at peace with God. That's what the Word says and that's what it means and that's what gives us peace.

Verse 2:
We give thanks to God always for you all, making mention of you in our prayers.

Paul gave thanks to God because he knew that it was by God's grace that there was a church in Thessalonica. Giving "thanks to God always" does not mean he was praying one hundred percent of the time; it simply means that every time they—Paul, Silas, and Timothy—thought of the Thessalonians, they thanked God for them. The word "for" in this verse is the word *para* which means to give thanks to God "along with" you; in other words "I give thanks to God," Paul says, "while you are thanking God, too, in Thessalonica."

Verse 3:
Remembering without ceasing your work of
faith [believing], and labour of love, and patience of hope in our Lord Jesus Christ, in the
sight of God and our Father.

The words "without ceasing" in this verse are
literally "with careful attention and perseverance."
Obviously, the expression "without ceasing" cannot
mean "all the time without stopping." We have to
sleep and eat sometimes, and take care of other
matters. Paul is telling the church at Thessalonica
that he is remembering with careful attention, with
perseverance, "your work of [genitive of origin,
'proceeding from'] faith [*pistis*, believing]...." Paul
looked at the church in Thessalonica and he could see
the work that was being accomplished as a result of
their believing. That's why he prayed for them with
careful attention and perseverance.

"Labour of love, and patience of hope" literally
is "loving labor and hopeful patience of our Lord
Jesus Christ." Paul is talking about their work proceeding from believing and their loving labor and
hopeful patience waiting for the Lord Jesus Christ.
The hope relates itself to something that could not
be had then, but which they were looking forward
to in the future, as recorded later in this epistle.

> I Thessalonians 2:19:
> For what *is* our hope, or joy, or crown of
> rejoicing? *Are* not even ye in the presence of
> our Lord Jesus Christ at his coming?

They looked for Christ's return, just as we do.
This is acting out of hope, anticipating that which
has not yet occurred.

That is why Paul calls the labor of the Thessalonian church "loving labor with hopeful patience."
They labored lovingly, holding forth God's Word
proceeding from their believing, hoping for the
return of Christ. This is exactly what we do today.
This record is as timely as if it had been written
today. Immediately upon this reference to the
hope, Paul reminds them of their sonship.

> I Thessalonians 1:4:
> Knowing, brethren beloved, your election of
> God.

Why are they beloved? Because they have grace,
they have been begotten of God, they are His children and therefore are beloved. The word "election"
simply means "chosen." Colossians 3:12 tells us,
"Put on therefore, as the elect of God [the chosen
of God]...." God called us and in His foreknowledge
He knew who would hear and accept. We were chosen

by God Almighty who created the heavens and the earth; who set the stars in their courses; who chose us before the foundation of the world. When we fully realize the greatness of being the elect, the called, the chosen of God, we readily accept what God says we are in Him.

> Verse 5:
> For our gospel came not unto you in word only, but also *[kai]* in power, and in the Holy Ghost, and in much assurance; as ye know what manner of men we were among you for your sake.

Greek always places the word "also," *kai,* before the word it emphasizes. A consistent English translation would place it after the word it emphasizes, so this verse actually reads, "Our gospel came to you not only in Word, but in power also and in the holy spirit." The gospel came unto them not only in word, but also in power, because the power was in the *pneuma hagion,* the holy spirit, God's gift in manifestation.

Anybody can *talk* about the gospel, but that is not the criterion for the truth of God's Word. There must be signs, miracles, and wonders along with the spoken Word or the talk is just talk. An example of what happens when the Word is preached is recorded in Acts 8.

109

Acts 8:5 and 6:
Then Philip went down to the city of Samaria,
and preached Christ unto them.
And the people with one accord gave heed
unto those things which Philip spake, hearing
and seeing the miracles which he did.

The people in Samaria believed Philip's teaching,
because they heard and saw the miracles which
Philip did. In I Thessalonians Paul talked about
these same kinds of signs, miracles, and wonders
when he says, "For our gospel came not unto you
in word only, but also in power, and in the Holy
Ghost, and in much assurance...." The assurance
that Paul gave them in this verse is the full assurance
of the understanding to the end that they acknowledged the mystery.

Colossians 2:2:
That their hearts might be comforted, being
knit together in love, and unto all riches of
the full assurance of understanding, to the
acknowledgement of the mystery of God, and
of the Father, and of Christ.

That assurance is the full assurance of the mystery:
God in Christ in you, the fullness of the gift of holy
spirit.

110

In I Thessalonians 1 Paul continues reminding the Thessalonians of how they had accepted God's Word.

Verse 6:
And ye became followers [*mimētēs*, imitators] of us, and of the Lord, having received the word in much affliction [in the midst of much affliction], with joy of the Holy Ghost.

The word "followers" is the Greek word *mimētēs* from which we get the word "mimic" in English. It means "imitators." Of course, here it is used in a very positive sense of copying or modeling oneself after someone else.

The people became imitators of Paul, Silas, and Timothy, and thus of the Lord. Why? Because that is a human reaction. People watch and imitate people. They look at us—how we present ourselves, how we act, what we say, how we dress. If you are going to catch fish, put good bait on the hook; if you are going to hold forth the Word of God, put on and act the Word. People have to see it in your face, your walk, your whole manner. You can't tell them, "Don't look at us; look at the Lord Jesus Christ." They can't see the Lord Jesus Christ, but they can see you. When Peter and John were going to the temple, according to Acts 3, and they had the revelation to

111

deliver the cripple at the Gate Beautiful, the first thing Peter said to the man was, "Look on us." They first had to get the man's attention, just as we have to get people's attention by holding forth the greatness of God's Word with all our personality, our drive, our conviction, and our distinctive appeal to make the beauty of that Word live.

As people get into the truth of God's Word, it takes time for them to jell its greatness to the point that they walk on it. They need time to mature in God's household and in the knowledge of His Word. In doing this they are to imitate the examples set by the men and women of God who are responsible to lead them. This does not mean that we take on our leaders' idiosyncrasies and faults. It means that as we learn principles in God's Word, we imitate those men and women *as we see them practice the truth*. It is a family learning situation, a growing experience. We learn from those who have been practicing the principles of God's Word longer than we have. In doing this we become more and more perfected in His Word. We become more and more like the Lord Jesus Christ. In turn, as God's children, we become more and more like our Heavenly Father, for we are learning to walk in the perfection to which He has called us. That is the pattern. We imitate the lives of those whom God has set in His household as leaders and overseers. They then imitate the Lord Jesus

Christ by walking faithfully on God's Word. As all of us do this, we are imitating the source of that Word, God. Paul sets this pattern of imitation very clearly in the first letter to the Corinthians.

> I Corinthians 4:15-17:
> For though ye have ten thousand instructors in Christ, yet *have ye* not many fathers: for in Christ Jesus I have begotten you through the gospel.
> Wherefore I beseech you, be ye followers [*mimētēs,* imitators] of me.
> For this cause have I sent unto you Timotheus, who is my beloved son, and faithful in the Lord, who shall bring you into remembrance of my ways which be in Christ, as I teach every where in every church.

As the man of God, Paul had fathered the Corinthians in the Word. He had taught them the Word and was their example. Therefore they were to imitate him. They could do this as Timothy, who was faithful in the Lord, brought to their remembrance Paul's ways in Christ. It was those ways in Christ that they were to imitate. Paul mentions their imitating him again later in I Corinthians.

> I Corinthians 11:1:
> Be ye followers [*mimētēs,* imitators] of me, even as I also *am* of Christ.

113

Paul imitated Christ as he walked steadfastly on God's Word. Because of his walk and his ministry, Paul was able to crystallize these great truths in Philippians.

Philippians 4:9:
Those things, which ye have both learned, and received, and heard, and seen in me, do: and the God of peace shall be with you.

As more and more people grew up to serve in positions of leadership in spreading God's truth, they also were acknowledged as great examples of the Word. They were faithful to God's Word; they imitated Paul as well as others who were living God's Word, then they in turn became examples to the Church.

In speaking of following other people's examples, there is a record in God's Word where an entire church in one area was told to imitate the churches in another area.

I Thessalonians 2:14:
For ye, brethren, became followers [*mimētēs,* imitators] of the churches of God which in Judea are in Christ Jesus....

Why did the church in Thessalonica imitate the churches in Judea? Because in both places the

114

churches had undergone similar experiences of persecution, and both were "in Christ Jesus." Yet it was the churches in Judea, which had lived God's Word for a longer period of time, that set the example.

All of these great principles are pointed to one goal: that we, by living God's Word faithfully, will be imitators of God.

> Ephesians 5:1:
> Be ye therefore followers [*mimētēs*, imitators] of God, as dear children.

What a wonderful truth! In an earthly family the children imitate the ways of their parents. As God's children we are to imitate Him. Because God is Spirit and cannot be seen, we can only do this by living the greatness of His Word. Only one person has ever done this perfectly, and that was the Lord Jesus Christ. He imitated God by perfectly carrying out God's Word. More and more we too can learn to walk that same way. God has given us a tremendous family in which to do it. We imitate those followers of Christ who are maturely applying and living this walk. While doing this, we continually study God's Word, put it on in our minds, and live it. As the Word prevails in our lives, we walk in unity in the

115

abundance of His Word as "imitators of God," our Father.

According to I Thessalonians 1:6, the church in Thessalonica had received God's Word in spite of the many afflictions that we read about in Acts 17. They remained faithful to the truth they had been taught by Paul, Silas, and Timothy. Now watch what happened.

> I Thessalonians 1:7 and 8:
> So that ye were ensamples to all that believe in Macedonia and Achaia.
> For from you sounded out [echoed] the word of the Lord not only in Macedonia and Achaia, but also in every place your faith [believing] to God-ward is spread abroad; so that we need not to speak any thing.

Paul said there was no need to say anything further about their believing because every one knew that they were examples. Because of the example of their believing, they sounded forth the Word of the Lord in every place. It was spread abroad. Certainly, there was some persecution, some affliction, but the Word was spread abroad because the people in Thessalonica believed and held it forth. Thessalonian believers had matured and, therefore, Thessalonica had become a major center for the Church.

Verse 9:

For they [those places which heard God's Word because of the Thessalonian church] themselves shew of us what manner of entering in we had unto you, and how ye turned to God from idols to serve the living and true God.

Paul and his helpers had turned the Thessalonians from idols to serve the living and true God. Anything we put before the God and Father of our Lord Jesus Christ is an idol. Only holding forth the greatness of God's Word will turn people from their idols "to serve the living and true God."

Verse 10:

And to wait for his Son from heaven, whom he raised from the dead, *even* Jesus, which delivered us from the wrath to come.

Even with all the believing that turns people from their idols to the true God, we still wait with hope, waiting for His Son from heaven whom He raised from the dead. As great as life is when we believe God's Word now, it will be even greater when Christ returns to gather us.

Some people propound that we have to go through the Revelation Period with all of the tribulation and wrath of that time before Christ will return. But

117

verse 10 plainly tells us that we are delivered from the wrath to come. That is God's unchangeable truth. Even Christians who *say* they are going through the tribulations and destruction of the Revelation Period are not going through it because the Word says they have already been delivered from it. The light afflictions of our time don't even slow us down because we are delivered and because we have joy in the holy spirit. We have the "sure" hope.

The church in Thessalonica stood strong. And as they stood strong, their influence reached out over that whole section of Asia Minor. They became rooted in this wonderful Word; they declared it with boldness, with loving labor, and with hopeful patience as they waited for the return of the Lord.

We can live victoriously when we become imitators of the Lord Jesus Christ and imitators of men and women of God who both talk and live the greatness of God's wonderful Word. We are followers of the one true way. As we look for the Lord Jesus Christ and wait for his return, the glory of the Lord will become written on our faces, our souls, our whole lives. He will become reflected by our entire, dynamic beings.

CHAPTER SEVEN

Abraham's Example of Believing

One day while standing at the feet of the statues in the town square in Worms, Germany, I pictured in my mind the days and times of Martin Luther, Melanchthon, John Knox, Calvin, and other men of the Reformation. Of course, it was Martin Luther who really fanned the flames when he nailed the 95 theses to the church door in Wittenberg and later when he stood in trial before the religious henchmen of his day. He declared boldly in front of them at the close of his defense, "Here I stand. God help me. I cannot do otherwise." It was Martin Luther who stood against the corruption of the institutionalized Christianity.

Luther was a Roman Catholic and his idea was simply to reform the Roman Catholic Church. But one person can never, in limited time, reform an established institution; it is impossible. Neither Jesus Christ nor God Almighty ever established an institution or a denomination, but God did establish the

119

truth of His Word and the fellowship of the like-minded believers who are called Christians in the Bible. If Martin Luther had been able to live another thirty, forty, sixty or one hundred years, he might have brought about a major reformation. The one of which he was a part was only a partial one. He did not live long enough and neither did Knox, Melanchthon, Calvin or Zwingli. Much of Protestanism today still has vestiges of its Roman Catholic background. But Martin Luther did see accurate principles from God's Word. One he saw is found in the Book of Romans which declares that man is justified by faith. Luther realized that salvation is not of works, but by faith and by the grace of God. Let us explore some of this greatness about righteousness and salvation in the Word from the fourth chapter of Romans.

Romans 4:1-3:

What shall we say then that Abraham our father, as pertaining to the flesh, hath found?

For if Abraham were justified by works, he hath *whereof* to glory; but not before God.

For what saith the scripture? Abraham believed God, and it [the believing] was counted unto him for righteousness.

This section in Romans is a reference to a passage in Genesis 15 which tells about God and His relationship with Abraham.

Genesis 15:6:
And he [Abraham] believed in the Lord; and he
[the Lord] counted it to him [Abraham] for
righteousness.

The word "believed" in Genesis 15:6 is the word
pisteuo in Romans 4:3. Now Abraham believed God
and it was counted or set to his account, for righteousness. Romans 4 continues, showing the difference between receiving righteousness by works and
righteousness by grace.

Romans 4:4:
Now to him that worketh [he that does good
works] is the reward not reckoned of grace,
but of debt.

If we work for something, we have earned what
we receive. Abraham didn't work for righteousness.
He believed God, and God did what? Counted it to
him or reckoned it unto him for righteousness.

Verses 5-7:
But to him that worketh not, but believeth on
him that justifieth the ungodly, his faith [believ-
ing] is counted for righteousness.
Even as David also describeth the blessedness of
the man, unto whom God imputeth righteousness without works,

> *Saying,* Blessed *are* they whose iniquities are forgiven, and whose sins are covered.

That is tremendous. Every time I read this kind of thing in the Word, especially in the Book of Romans, my mind remembers I John 1:9 where it says, "If we confess our sins, he [God] is faithful and just to forgive us *our* sins, and to cleanse us from all unrighteousness." In contrast to us in the Age of Grace, Abraham was not cleansed. His sins were only covered. Why were the Old Testament people not cleansed? The cleansing was not available until Jesus Christ came. So what did God do before Jesus Christ made the cleansing available? By their believing God, God counted or reckoned unto them righteousness. However, their sins were simply covered, not cleansed. That is a major difference between the Old Testament and the Church to which you and I belong. In the Old Testament when man believed God, God reckoned righteousness and covered man's sins.

You may say it doesn't make any difference, but it surely does. The covering of sin is simply like taking a garbage can full of spoiled leftovers and putting the lid on it. In the Age of the Church of the Body to which you and I belong, we receive not a covering of our sin, but a cleansing from sin. We are washed out with God's spiritual detergent. That which God had wrought in Christ Jesus was so tremendous that sin was all washed away, not simply covered.

122

Verses 8-10:

Blessed *is* the man to whom the Lord will not impute sin.

Cometh this blessedness then upon the circumcision *only*, or upon the uncircumcision also? for we say that faith [believing] was reckoned to Abraham for righteousness.

How was it then reckoned [unto Abraham]? when he was in circumcision [after he was circumcised], or in uncircumcision? Not in circumcision, but in uncircumcision.

Righteousness wasn't reckoned unto Abraham after he was circumcised, but while he was still uncircumcised. The record we read in Genesis 15:6 came before the circumcision of Abraham, which is recorded in Genesis 17.

Verse 11:

And he [Abraham] received the sign of circumcision [after he was righteous], a seal of the righteousness of the faith [believing] which *he had yet* being uncircumcised....

Abraham was circumcised as a seal or symbol of his receiving righteousness from God.

Verses 11 and 12:

...that he [Abraham] might be the father of all them that believe, though they be not circumcised; that righteousness might be imputed unto them also.

And the father of circumcision to them who are not of the circumcision only, but who also walk in the steps of that faith [believing] of our father Abraham, which *he had* being *yet* uncircumcised.

The whole statement which God is setting forth in His Word is that it was not for Abraham's works, such as circumcision, that Abraham received righteousness, because Abraham did works after he was made righteous. The same holds true for us. We are saved by grace, "...not of works lest any man should boast."

Verses 13 and 14:

For the promise, that he [Abraham] should be the heir of the world, *was* not to Abraham, or to his seed, through the law, but through the righteousness of faith [believing].

For if they which are of the law *be* heirs, faith [believing] is made void, and the promise made of none effect.

The law didn't bring righteousness. Believing did. Why? Read the next verse.

Verse 15:
Because the law worketh wrath: for where
no law is, *there is* no transgression.

You cannot have a transgression until you have a
law. In other words, if there is no stop sign, you
cannot break the law that says you must stop for
a stop sign. There has to be a law before a person
can break it.

Verse 16:
Therefore *it* [righteousness] *is* of faith, that
it might be by grace; to the end the promise
might be sure to all the seed [the believers];
not to that only which is of the law, but to
that also which is of the faith [believing] of
Abraham; who is the father of us all [who
believe].

As the one to whom the promises were made,
Abraham believed God and became the father of all
who would believe, both of the circumcision and the
uncircumcision. His believing made it possible for
God to reckon righteousness unto him. When we
believed to be saved, Abraham became our father
and we also, as he did, received righteousness. However, this righteousness which we received was not
just reckoned to us, as it was to Abraham. Our
righteousness is born within for we have received

the righteousness of God in Christ, and we have Christ in us the hope of glory.*

Now that we are born again, we have the seed from God in Christ in us which is the gift of holy spirit. Christ was of the seed of Abraham, both according to his flesh and by his believing. And now God has created Christ in us on account of our believing. Therefore, it is by believing that we are of the seed of Abraham.

> Verse 17:
> (As it is written, I have made thee [Abraham] a father of many nations,) before him whom he believed, *even* God, who quickeneth the dead, and calleth those things which be not as though they were.

God promised Abraham he would be the father of many nations. Abraham never saw it come to pass in his lifetime. That is why the word "hope" is used in verse 18.

---

*II Corinthians 5:21: "For he [God] hath made him [Jesus] *to be* sin for us, who knew no sin; that we might be made the righteousness of God in him [Christ]."
Colossians 1:27: "To whom God would make known what *is* the riches of the glory of this mystery among the Gentiles; which is Christ in you, the hope of glory."

Verse 18:
Who [Abraham] against hope believed in hope
[in the hope that it would come to pass, he
believed] ....

The Word says that if you are born again of God's
Spirit, then Christ is coming back for you. God is
going to give you a body fashioned like unto Jesus
Christ's glorious, resurrected body. That is our hope.
I have no problem with that. I have no problem with
the resurrection or the return of Christ, because that's
no more difficult than trying to figure out how I
got here the first time out of a minute ovum and
sperm. Do you really think that the same God who
made those natural laws cannot give us new bodies
when Christ returns? Your father and mother got
you here the first time. I'm pretty sure that God is
more capable than your parents. We really don't
have to accept God's Word by blind faith as some
people suggest we do. The God of the Bible is a
God of law and order. He is a God of cause and effect,
and you and I can know that we know that we know
we are born again. We can know that we are heaven-
bound. Don't let anyone tell you that you must
"accept it by faith." That is contrary to the Word.
Abraham knew better than that. God said He would
make Abraham a father of many nations. Abraham
had hoped that this would come to pass, and he

127

simply kept believing. We, likewise, have this same kind of hope for Christ's return.

> Verse 18:
> Who against hope believed in hope, that he might become the father of many nations; according to that which was spoken [by whom? *By* God to Abraham], So shall thy seed [the believers] be.

Abraham never saw God's promise come to pass, but he steadfastly believed God. Abraham devised and put into operation his own plans in trying to carry out God's promise that he would be the father of many nations. Abraham tried to have a son by Hagar. I can appreciate this plan of Abraham. He was being so typically human. He was trying to help God out, give Him a little assistance. But finally Abraham got around to trusting God in this matter of physical fatherhood when he was 99, close to 100. The next verse in Romans 4 continues speaking of Abraham.

> Verse 19:
> And being not weak in faith [believing], he [Abraham] considered not his own body now dead, when he was about an hundred years old, neither yet the deadness of Sara's womb.

God had told Abraham He was going to give him seed and Abraham said, "Sara is not doing so well." So for many years he used his sense-knowledge and tried to figure out how he could help fulfill God's promise. At last Abraham got around to believing that what God said He meant. I thank God when anybody gets around to believing. I don't care if he is 99; I don't care if he is 16. I just thank God when people finally get to the place that they believe, because when they start to believe they get results from their believing just as Abraham did.

The promise which was made to Abraham, said that God would make Abraham's seed like the sand of the seas, like the multitude of the stars. Even though Abraham did not have one child, God said He would make Abraham's offspring beyond counting. And He meant He would do it. So when Abraham was 99 and Sara about 90, a son by the name of Isaac came along. That is what the next verse speaks of.

Verse 20:
He [Abraham] staggered not at the promise of God through unbelief; but was strong in faith [believing], giving glory to God.

Abraham simply praised God. He said, "God, I just thank you for bringing this promise to pass."

129

Verse 21:
And being fully persuaded that, what he [God]
had promised, he [God] was able also to perform.

This verse contains the key to believing. Believing
is not just a mental process; it is complete persuasion.
Believing is being convinced of God's Word beyond
a shadow of doubt even if you never see it come to
pass. It is still God's Word, and it will have to come
to pass sometime. That is truly believing. All through
the years, Abraham was working on the promise of
God and finally got to the place that he believed
that he believed that he believed, and he knew
beyond a shadow of a doubt that God's promise
would be realized. That is being fully persuaded.
What was he fully persuaded about? That what
God promised God was able to perform and He
would perform.

Verse 22:
And therefore it was imputed to him for righteousness.

There it is—as plain as day. "Therefore it [Abra-
ham's believing] was imputed to him for righteousness."

Verses 23-25:

Now it was not written for his sake alone, that it was imputed to him;

But for us also, to whom it shall be imputed, if we believe on him that raised up Jesus our Lord from the dead;

Who [Jesus] was delivered [to the cross, was delivered to death] for our offences, and was raised again for our justification [when we were justified].

Then when Jesus Christ died, what about my sins? What about my offenses? What about my iniquities? What about my enmity against God? Where did they go? They died with Jesus Christ. He took it upon himself.

Jesus Christ was delivered for our offences and was raised from the dead when we were justified. That is it. Delivered for our offences and raised from the dead when our justification was accomplished. And that was after spending three days and three nights in the grave. The whole law was fulfilled because Christ was the end of the law. That is what Isaiah was talking about when he wrote, "All we like sheep have gone astray; we have turned every one to his own way; and the Lord hath laid on him [the Messiah] the iniquity of us all." Well, if God put on Jesus the iniquity of us all and then he bore our sins,

131

where is our sin? It is on him. Praise the Lord! God have mercy on those people who want to carry their own sins. They have a load on their back, I guarantee you. A person's sin would burden anyone down. Out of ignorance these poor souls do not realize what God really did in Christ. When God's Word talks about salvation by grace, there are no "buts." When Christ died, he died; when he became sin, he became sin; and when God raised him from the dead we were justified.

Romans 5:1:
Therefore being justified by faith, we have peace with God through our Lord Jesus Christ.

When we confessed Jesus as Lord and believed God raised him from the dead, we were saved. By that simple act of believing, God's grace made us whole. God's Word says we were justified. And because of this, we have peace with God, made possible by the works of our Lord Jesus Christ.

What a message to our time! Everybody talks about peace. But there is no true peace without the prince of peace. How in the world can we have peace until Christ is settled in the innermost resources of our souls and we have renewed our minds to know that we *have* and we *are* what the Word of God says we have and are? It says we have peace. So when the whole world around us is peaceless, what do we have? Peace. When the old ship of life rocks and rolls, what do we have? Peace. We have peace with God. That is what a man needs today. That is what man's soul is really hungering for. That is why he is looking in all the other fountains, but he cannot satisfy the thirst. Only truth quenches thirst.

> Romans 5:1 and 2:
> Therefore being justified by faith, we have peace with God through our Lord Jesus Christ: By whom [the Lord Jesus Christ] also we have access by faith into this grace wherein we stand, and rejoice in hope of the glory of God.

The second usage of the words "by faith" must be deleted because they are not found in the oldest texts. This should read, "By whom [Jesus Christ] we have access also into this grace wherein we stand...." Because of what Christ did for us, we stand in grace. I know of no other way to stand than in grace, God's divine favor. People who think our stand and our approval comes because of good works never stand. They are always bowed over with this burden. But we not only stand, we rejoice. We "...rejoice in hope of the glory of God."

> Verse 3:
> And not only *so,* but we glory in tribulations also....

133

That doesn't mean we seek after tribulations. But if the Devil loads it on us, because of people's unbelief, we don't complain about it. Do you know why?

Verse 3:
...knowing that tribulation [which the Devil heaps on us] worketh patience.

Tribulation makes us stand. If we never had an enemy, we wouldn't know what it is to stand. We would have no opportunity. That is the challenge of tribulation.

Verses 4 and 5:
And patience, [worketh] experience; and experience, hope:
And hope maketh not ashamed; because the love of God is shed abroad in our hearts by the Holy Ghost *[pneuma hagion]* which is [was] given unto us.

Do we have the holy spirit? God said He gave it to us. So by it, the holy spirit, the love of God is shed abroad in our hearts.

Verses 6-9:
For when we were yet without strength, in due time Christ died for the ungodly.

134

For scarcely for a righteous man will one die: yet peradventure for a good man some would even dare to die.

But God commendeth his love toward us, in that, while we were yet sinners [dead in trespasses and sins, without God and without hope], Christ died for us.

Much more then, being now justified by his [Jesus Christ's] blood, we shall [absolutely] be saved from wrath through him.

Do you know what it means to be saved from wrath? The Book of Revelation gives some information about the time of wrath. Some Christians teach that we Christians must go through the tribulation period. They get this idea from the word "tribulation" in Romans 5:3. Well, we don't need to live in the times of the Book of Revelation to get tribulation, because some people will make sure we get a little tribulation now. There is a difference between tribulation and wrath. Romans 5:9 says we shall be saved from the wrath through Jesus Christ. That is what it says and that is what it means. We are now justified by his blood. That is why we are saved now. We are not going through the wrath period. It doesn't matter whether the Lord comes today or a hundred years from now. We still would not go through the wrath period because we're saved from it and the time of wrath hasn't yet come. It is going to start *after* the gathering together of the Church of the Body. Let the unbelievers stay around; we are going to take a better route together.

> Verse 10:
> For if, when we were enemies, we were reconciled to God by the death of his Son, much more, being reconciled, we shall be saved by his life.

In verse 9 we were told we are justified, and in verse 10 we see we are reconciled. These are two great words with tremendously deep meaning for all of us. To be justified means to be freed from blame, to be declared guiltless. To reconcile means to bring back together from having been separated. Man, after Adam's fall, was separated from God; but now, in Christ Jesus, we are reconciled—brought back together—with God.

> Verse 11:
> And not only *so*, but we also joy in God through our Lord Jesus Christ, by whom we have now received the atonement.

"Joy" is another great word. When we know we are justified and reconciled, we really have joy. We "joy in God through our Lord Jesus Christ [who accomplished it for us], by whom we have now received the atonement." Isn't that a tremendous truth!

What we have read is just part of the great truths of Romans. We have received justification by the blood of Jesus Christ and reconciliation through Christ. The whole thing is taken care of by Christ Jesus. You and I are born again of God's Spirit, Jesus Christ being our surety. The Word of God says we are not saved by works; we are saved by grace. Abraham's righteousness was given to him because of his believing, not because of his works—and so is ours.

Part III

God's Strength in Us

Part III

God's Strength in Us

Both the studies which make up this section stress the strength which God has put in each of us, His children. When we look at ourselves from a senses point of view, we may feel small and insignificant. But this is a deception to men and women who are born again of God's seed. We have been given God's sufficiency. So we look not at ourselves, but at God and the promises of His Word.

When we look at our flesh, we see "earthen vessels"—simple, corruptible "clay pots." But the power inside is the power of God. Such a combination God chose: our earthen vessels filled with God's power! God is constantly trying to raise our vision away from ourselves and unto Him. What a level at which to live! What strength indeed we have, because God is our strength and sufficiency.

CHAPTER EIGHT

God Is Our Sufficiency

From time to time those of us who have been deeply moved by God's Word try to find words in our vocabulary to express how we feel within our hearts for God's goodness to us. As workmen we have studied God's Word. We have seen that the Pauline epistles are such informative and uplifting revelations. These epistles reveal the significance of what was brought about because of Jesus Christ's sacrifice of himself. We could study the gospels until we were exhausted, but we would never find revealed the greatness that Christ was our substitute. We see this only in the epistles. We would never see the reality of the new creation within each of us believers in the gospels. Again, it is in the epistles. In the gospels we do not see the ministry of Jesus Christ for the saints at the right hand of God; it is the epistles that show the ministry of Jesus Christ as he is now seated with God.

During the Gospel Period, people had no spirit so the body-and-soul believers could only observe life from a senses point of view. Men in the gospels

141

asked Jesus as recorded in John 6:30, "What sign shewest thou then, that we may see, and believe thee?" Time and time again inquirers asked for tangible proof. Thomas insisted, "Except I shall see in his hands the print of the nails...I will not believe." In the gospels, people had to see in order to believe. But the Church epistles establish the order that a person first believes and then he sees. Thus you and I do not first see and then believe; we first believe God's Word and then we see the truth of it bear fruit in our lives as we walk on it.

Another critical difference between the time of the gospels and the time of the epistles pertains to power. In the gospels, the people were overwhelmed at the miracles that Jesus Christ did. They stood in utter amazement at the power he had. In the gospels it was Jesus Christ who controlled devil spirits; he delivered people from sickness; he raised the dead. The information that believers have God-given power comes like a thunderbolt in the Church epistles. In the gospels we see Jesus Christ as the conqueror. We never see the revelation in the gospels that we also, as born-again believers, are more than conquerors, that we are to be filled with all the fullness of God. This revelation is given in the epistles, and the epistles are addressed to us. They are addressed to the Church of Grace which began on the day of Pentecost.

142

There is only one true God, and that God can only be known from His Word. A person cannot get the knowledge of God from any other source than God's Word. I learned this from twenty years of experience in reading around the Word. I once read what every current book said, every popular magazine said, and every major theologian said. I had negatively positioned my mind to the point that I didn't even believe that the word "Holy" should be on the Bible cover. So I know most of the arguments against the reality of God's Word; I've been there. But having come to the position of accepting God's Word as His will, I have something to say to our generation that is absolutely true and that is absolutely sure: No man can know God's will without knowing His Word.

In understanding that God is our sufficiency, there is a basic truth in God's Word which we believers must realize. That truth is that God has given us all things necessary for an abundant life. Look at II Corinthians 3:5.

> Not that we are sufficient of ourselves to think any thing as of ourselves; but our sufficiency *is* of God.

That is what it says and that is what it means. Now if I declare anything other than what the Word says, either God's Word is lying or I am. It is as simple as

143

that. Perhaps I don't feel that my sufficiency is of God. That makes it no less of God. Feelings do not validate or invalidate God or His Word. Feelings come and go, but the Word of God lives and abides forever. When you begin to believe the Word, then the manifestation of the greatness of the spirit from God becomes a reality.

According to II Corinthians 3:5, our sufficiency is of whom? "Of God." Not that we would think anything of ourselves, but God is our sufficiency. Our sufficiency is not of ourselves; it is not of any other individual; it is of God.

If God says we have *His* sufficiency, how much do we have? His sufficiency. I would say that more sufficiency than that is impossible to come by. Now what does God's sufficiency include? Ephesians 1:6 tells us part of it.

> To the praise of the glory of his grace, wherein he hath made us accepted in the beloved.

The Bible says God has made us accepted. Well, if I'm going to be sufficient, I have to be accepted by God. It has nothing to do with my feelings; He simply caused me to become this way. In Christ Jesus I came from God's spiritual factory having what God says I have. He made me accepted. Since that is what the Bible says, that is what it means. Isn't that wonderful? Ephesians 1 further explains how we are sufficient.

Ephesians 1:7 and 8:
In whom we have redemption through his blood, the forgiveness [remission] of sins, according to the riches of his grace;
Wherein he hath abounded toward us in all wisdom and prudence.

Besides being redeemed, we also have been accepted, and we have received remission of sins. All of these qualities contribute to our sufficiency.

Ephesians 1:9 and 18:
Having made known unto us the mystery of his will, according to his good pleasure which he hath purposed in himself:
The eyes of your understanding being enlightened; that ye may know what is the hope of his calling, and what the riches of the glory of his inheritance in the saints.

We are also to know the hope of His calling and the greatness of our inheritance from God. There is another translation which says we should "enjoy our share of the inheritance." In order to enjoy our share of the inheritance, we must first of all, find out how much that inheritance is, and then we have to develop the ability to use it wisely. The second chapter of Ephesians unfolds more of these great truths.

Ephesians 2:6:
And [God] hath raised *us* up together, and made *us* sit together in heavenly *places* in Christ Jesus.

Even while we are here on earth as ambassadors, as far as God is concerned, we are already seated in the heavenlies. God has already placed us in the heavenlies while we are yet working down here. That is good spiritual insurance. It is a tremendous guarantee. Should we be discouraged? Why, if nobody believed God's Word, it is still God's Word, and I'm still seated in the heavenlies. I want to tell you, we cannot lose.

Ephesians 2:19:
Now therefore ye are no more strangers and foreigners, but fellowcitizens with the saints, and of the household of God.

This is part of our sufficiency which is of God. Isn't it wonderful to belong to God and His household? We've got blue-ribbon credentials.

I am still choosing a few of the scriptures that demonstrate the sufficiency which we Church members have.

Colossians 1:12:
Giving thanks unto the Father, which hath made us meet [adequate, sufficient] to be partakers of the inheritance of the saints in light.

God has made us adequate to share in His inheritance. He made us sufficient. Isn't that wonderful?

Colossians 1:13:
[God] Who hath delivered [past tense] us [rescued us] from the power of darkness, and hath translated *us* [given us citizenship] into the kingdom [by the work] of his dear Son [or "by the love of His Son"].

God has delivered us, rescued us, from the power of darkness. We are delivered and given citizenship in His kingdom.

Colossians 1:14:
In whom we have redemption through his blood, *even* the forgiveness [remission] of sins.

God casts our sins from us as far as the east is from the west and as deep as the deepest sea, and He will

147

remember them no more. So if God Almighty, who gave me sonship, refuses to remember my sins, then I've got to be foolish to continue remembering them. I shouldn't want to live below par when God has made it possible for me to be more than a conqueror. This certainly would be a tremendous contradiction of the revelation addressed to the Church. Look at Colossians 2:10.

> And ye are complete in him, which [who] is the head of all principality and power.

We are complete in Christ Jesus. Well, if we are complete, we are not lacking even one thing, we are sufficient. If we lacked one thing, we would be deficient instead of sufficient.

The reason I have all these good things is that God gave them to me. I am what the Word of God says I am. And it says I am—we are—complete. So how can a Christian pray, "O Lord, give me this, give me that"? Our God has already made everything available in Christ Jesus. When we were born again of God's Spirit, we received God in Christ in us, the hope of glory. That is the completeness. Our prayer of believing is simply one of thanking God for what He has already given us according to our knowledge of His Word. When we thank Him for what is already available, our request is filled and comes into manifes-

148

tation in our lives. We are complete in Christ Jesus. We've got to start walking with that completeness— not by the letter of the law but the spirit of life, which is the love of God shed abroad in our hearts. This walk includes living with tenderness, peace, love, forgiveness, and understanding.

What we look at is what we become. If I am with people who are always negative, I will be influenced by that negativism. If a person lives long enough with people who have ticks, that person will eventually get ticks too. But if a person immerses his mind in the Lord Jesus Christ, he'll move from glory to glory. He will reflect the greatness of Christ within. Then a lot of these things which obstruct most people will just fall by the wayside, and life will begin to have a joy and a glow to it.

The glory walk is more than an earthly existence where we endure life's troubles just because we want to try to live through another day of confusion. Rather, life becomes a time for thanksgiving, a time of joy, and a time of blessing, because we are changed into what we look at which is the Lord Jesus Christ and what he accomplished for us and in us. Then we become as he is and manifest what he is. We hold forth the greatness of God's Word which is contained in the revelation addressed to the Church. Remember the little old poem:

God's Strength in Us

> God has no hands but our hands
> With which to give them bread.
> He has no feet but our feet with
>   which to move among the
>   almost dead.
> We say that we are His and He is
>   ours—
> Deeds are the proof of that, not words
> And these are the proving hours.

God wants us to exude the beauty of Christ which is in us so that we can enjoy life and so will others who observe us and who choose to walk in that same deliverance. This we are able to do, because God is our sufficiency.

CHAPTER NINE

We Have This Treasure in Earthen Vessels

Few Christians have ever come to an awareness of the greatness of their position in Christ. Lack of this knowledge has caused many of them to live far below par. They have magnified their own weaknesses and shortcomings above the greatness of what God made them when they received Christ in them, the hope of glory.*

II Corinthians contains a passage which sometimes seems like a paradox. On one hand we know that the Word teaches certain positive things that we as believers are, but then we read a scripture like verse 7 in II Corinthians 4.

II Corinthians 4:7:
But we have this treasure in earthen vessels....

---

*Colossians 1:27: "To whom God would make known what *is* the riches of the glory of this mystery among the Gentiles; which is Christ in you, the hope of glory."

God's Strength in Us

The point that has already been emphasized from this verse is that we are frail like earthen vessels. Through the years we have been taught that we are just poor Christians and told, "Well, we can't do very much because we're just simple earthen vessels." But there is more to this verse than that. Look at the rest of that verse.

> ...that the excellency of the power may be of God, and not of us.

Now we are cognizant of a great reality. I simply believe that I am what the Word says I am; I believe I have what the Word of God says I have; I believe I will be what the Word of God says I will be. And I believe that I have the power that the Word of God says I have even though I am an earthen vessel. The critical factor is that the excellency of the power in us is not of ourselves, but of God. Our excellency is of God and He is within us through Christ.

Now to make the greatness of this wonderful verse of truth come alive, we need to view it in context. So I would like to go back two chapters to II Corinthians 2.

> II Corinthians 2:14:
> Now thanks *be* unto God, which [who] always [not just once in a while, but always] causeth us to triumph in Christ....

152

Then don't let anybody come around and tell you that you as a Christian have to be downtrodden, that you have to be filled with worry, anxiety, fear and frustration; those negatives have to be for somebody else, not us, because God *always* causes us to triumph. And when you triumph, you triumph. When the winners' trophies are passed out, you receive one, for you have won, you have triumphed.

God's Word says that God always causes us to triumph. Now is God a liar or did He tell the truth? You have to become so convinced that the Word of God is the will of God that you just believe what it says. Then the Word can start coming into fruition, into manifestation, into concretion, in your life. God's Word never comes into concretion until we say what His Word says and we act on it.

A lot of people may speak those words, but then they don't act accordingly. They mentally assent to what God's Word says, yet they add the word "but." There can be no "but's" about it. When God said it, He meant it, and that settles it. God always causes us to triumph in Christ.

II Corinthians 2:14:
Now thanks *be* unto God, which always causeth us to triumph in Christ, and maketh manifest [brings into evidence] the savour of his knowledge by us in every [without exception] place.

153

Glory, what a ministry! The word "savour" is "fragrance." God makes manifest the fragrance, the sweet odor, of His knowledge. The moment we walk out on the Word, we exude a sweet fragrance with which no costly perfume can compare. But the key is that this fragrance of the knowledge of God has to be manifested by us. We are the ones who have to tell this knowledge, we have to hold it forth, we have to share it and live it. Then that knowledge is the sweetest fragrance in absolutely every place. That is God's Word!

> II Corinthians 2:15 and 16:
> For we are unto God a sweet savour [fragrance] of Christ, in them that are saved [being made whole], and in them that perish [are perishing]:
> To the one [the unbeliever who is perishing] *we are* the savour [Here the usage is "smell" or "odor."] of death unto death; and to the other [the believer who is being made whole] the savour of life unto life....

To those people on the outside who will not believe God's Word, we stink because they don't want to believe the Word of God. They don't even want to hear it. But, on the other hand, for those who will be saved and those who are saved, we are a fragrance of life. God gave us life in Christ Jesus. He changed us. He took us out of hell and set us on the road to heaven. Even though we are earthen vessels, the excellency of the power is still of God. But without that earthen vessel there would be no power in manifestation. God needs us to manifest His Word and power.

After II Corinthians 2:16 describes our smell of death to death and life to life, it ends with, "...And who *is* sufficient for these things?"

Well, who is sufficient for these things? We are. That is right. It isn't a question that has a negative answer, such as, "Nobody is sufficient or really capable." That is not what the Word says. It simply asks, "Who is sufficient for these things?" Well, we are. Why? Because inside our earthen vessel is God in Christ in us. Our sufficiency is not of our own doing. It states this in the third chapter of II Corinthians 3.

II Corinthians 3:5:
Not that we are sufficient of ourselves to think any thing as of ourselves; but our sufficiency *is* of God.

Isn't that wonderful! Our sufficiency comes from God. Bless your heart, how big is our God? Then how sufficient is our sufficiency? It must be sufficiently sufficient. That it is. This is what God says in His Word. Sufficient is what we are; sufficiency is what we have.

Returning to the second chapter of II Corinthians, we read how a believer smells like death to the unbeliever and like life to the believer. The context continues.

II Corinthians 2:17:
For we are not as many, which corrupt the word of God: but as of sincerity, but as of God, in the sight of God speak we in Christ.

For we are not as many, which [who] corrupt the word of God...." There must have been a little corruption in the days of the Apostle Paul. Times haven't changed. This word "corrupt" literally means "to adulterate": "For we are not as many who have adulterated the Word of God...."

Now the word "adulterated" is interesting. It is used in Greek literature when a tavern-keeper watered down or diluted the wine. "We are not as many who have watered down the Word of God." That is what some people were doing. Paul is referring to those who were diluting the greatness of God's Word. That really speaks clearly like a clarion horn. Most of so-called Christianity has devitalized the greatness of God's Word to being nothing but religious formalities or emotionalism. Few have come to understand and teach the Word in its integrity and power. As a result most Christians have led very defeated lives with little understanding of the greater realities of life. Sometimes we may think the Word ought to be watered down a little because it's just too good to be true. Well, in reality, it is so good that it *is* true. We cannot settle for half of the Word of God. It is either God's Word or it isn't. We don't add impurities. We just speak what God said and what God did. That is what it says: no diluting.

II Corinthians 3:1 and 2:

Do we begin again to commend ourselves? or need we, as some *others,* epistles of commendation to you, or *letters* of commendation from you?

Ye are our epistle written in our hearts, known and read of all men.

People who are born again of God's Spirit and who hold forth God's Word are epistles. We are living epistles. People read our lives, they see us. We are "known and read of all men." Most people never crack the cover of God's Book; even if they did, they wouldn't understand it. So do you know what they *are* going to read? They are going to read your life and my life, your actions and my actions. They are going to observe us. Where do we stand? What do we say? How do we act? Are we the epitomization of love or do we just talk about it? A short poem I once found summarizes this.

We are writing a gospel; a chapter each day,

By the deeds that we do; by the words that we say.
People read what we write, whether faithless or true.

Say! What is the gospel according to YOU?

We are what is "known and read of all men."

> II Corinthians 3:3-6:
> *Forasmuch as ye are* manifestly declared to be
> the epistle of Christ ministered by us, written
> not with ink, but with the Spirit of the living
> God; not in tables of stone, but in fleshy tables
> of the heart.
> And such trust have we through Christ to
> God-ward:
> Not that we are sufficient of ourselves to think
> any thing as of ourselves; but our sufficiency
> *is* of God;
> Who also hath made us able ministers of the
> new testament [by a new covenant] ....

The thing that makes us able ministers is the
enablement. It is that spirit within us from the living
God that is our enablement; this enablement makes
it possible for us to minister effectively.

> II Corinthians 3:6:
> Who also hath made us able ministers of the
> new testament; not of the letter, but of the

spirit: for the letter killeth, but the spirit giveth
life.

The letter of the law is what Paul is talking about.
He is talking in context about "tables of stone."
Well, what tables of stone were written? The ten
commandments. Moses brought them down from the
mountain, and then had to go up for a second set.
"[God has] made us able ministers by a new covenant; not [ministers] of the letter [of the law], but
of the spirit: for the letter [the law] killeth, but the
spirit giveth life." Any person who puts himself back
under the law gets killed in the process. Under the
law they must work and live according to the flesh,
their five senses. Romans 8 says, "For to be carnally
[fleshly] minded *is* death...." In doing this they
live below par and never manifest the effulgence of
the glory of the presence of Christ within.

Romans 10:4 says that Christ is the end of the law
to everyone who believes. If he is the end, he is the
end. If someone wants to be put under the law,
God's Word already tells us what is going to happen
to them. They are just going to die. For there is no
life in that law. Life is in the Spirit of God in Christ
in the believer.

II Corinthians 3:7 and 8:
But [in contrast] if the ministration [or admin-
istration] of death [talking about the law,

159

tables of stone], written *and* engraven in stones, was glorious, so that the children of Israel could not stedfastly behold the face of Moses for the glory of his countenance; which *glory* was to be done away:

How shall not the ministration [administration] of the spirit be rather [more] glorious?

We ought to be lit up like fluorescent bulbs. Moses came down from the mountain with the ten commandments on two tables of stone, holding the glory of that administration of the law in his hands. The reflection upon Moses' face from those stones on which those ten commandments were written was so great that the people could not look on his countenance. They had to cover their eyes and squint to look at his face. If that law which the Word says killeth was so bright, what about the administration in which we now live? Even though it was so glorious that the children of Israel couldn't look on Moses' face, that glory is nothing in comparison with the glory that excels in the Grace Administration, since the day of Pentecost, in which you and I live. That is tremendous! I didn't write the Book, and I didn't die for you, and I didn't bring it to pass. But, this is what God's Word says, and it is as plain as can be.

"How shall not the ministration of the spirit be more glorious?" That is why you shine. "Living epistles," remember? We radiate, we effervesce, we glow. Christ in us makes us bubble. That is what we have in the spirit. Isn't that beautiful?

II Corinthians 3:9-15:

For if the ministration of condemnation *be* glory, much more doth the ministration of righteousness exceed in glory.

For even that which was made glorious had no glory in this respect, by reason of the glory that excelleth.

For if that which is done away [the law] *was* glorious, much more that which remaineth *is* glorious.

Seeing then that we have such hope, we use great plainness of speech:

And not as Moses, *which* put a vail over his face, that the children of Israel could not stedfastly look to the end of that which is abolished:

But their minds were blinded: for until this day remaineth the same vail untaken away in the reading of the old testament; which *vail* is done away in Christ.

But even unto this day, when Moses is read, the vail is upon their heart.

Those people who were still putting themselves under the law could never see God's Word rightly divided to the Church of the Body. You cannot see the Age of Grace through the law; you have to see it through Christ Jesus.

> II Corinthians 3:16:
> Nevertheless when it [their heart] shall turn to the Lord, the vail shall be taken away.

Then our eyes will have unobstructed vision and see clearly.

> II Corinthians 3:17:
> Now the Lord is that Spirit: and where the Spirit of the Lord *is,* there *is* liberty.

We talk about people being set free! The Spirit of the Lord sets us at liberty from the law. "Where the Spirit of the Lord *is,* there *is* liberty."

> II Corinthians 3:18:
> But we all, with open face [without a veil] beholding as in a glass [mirror] the glory of the Lord, [and] are changed into the same image from glory to glory, *even* as by the Spirit of the Lord.

That is what I call the glory walk. We become what we look at. If we look at miseries and fears, what will we reflect? This is a rule which works with absolute reliability for saint and sinner alike. It has nothing to do with being a Christian or non-Christian. We are changed into the same image as we behold. As we look at the Lord Jesus Christ, we become a reflection of the glory of Christ. It is written all over our faces; it is written in our lives. We are changed into the same image, and it is from glory to glory. If today is good, just think of how good tomorrow is going to be! Our lives become more glorious each day.

II Corinthians 4:1:
Therefore seeing we have this ministry...

We do not have to beg God for His ministry; we do not have to attend a theological seminary to get it. The Word of God says we already have the ministry.

II Corinthians 4:1-5:
Therefore seeing we have this ministry, as we have received mercy, we faint not;
But [we] have renounced the hidden things of dishonesty, not walking in craftiness, nor handling the word of God deceitfully [by adulterating it]; but by manifestation of the truth commending ourselves to every man's

conscience in the sight of God.
But if our gospel be hid [veiled], it is hid [veiled] to them that are lost [perishing]:
In whom the god of this world hath blinded the minds of them which believe not, lest the light of the glorious gospel of Christ, who is the image of God, should shine unto them.
For we preach not ourselves, but Christ Jesus the Lord; and ourselves your servants for Jesus' sake.

We don't go around in the community and say, "Look, I know it all." No, we don't preach ourselves; we preach Christ Jesus. Of course, God has to communicate His will by way of His Word to a person, and that person has to carry through on the knowledge received. For example, when we are out witnessing, we are doing the witnessing. But we do not preach ourselves or another person or an organization; we preach God's Word. We hold forth the Word, which is Christ Jesus.

"And ourselves your servants for Jesus' sake" shows that we are servants to the fellow-believers. We are sons in our relationship with God, but we are servants to our fellowmen. I am your servant; I have to let you lean on me until you learn to walk; I have to give you milk until you get to the meat stage. Wherever you go, remember you are a servant to your fellowmen.

People have to depend on you until they grow strong enough to walk on God's Word on their own. We are a family. You have to care for the spiritual children with real patience and wisdom. If you're caring for a baby, would you give him a knife, a fork, and a beautiful linen napkin on an expensive linen tablecloth? Of course not. So, if we slowly nurture our physical children, what about our spiritual children? We have to bottle-feed them too. We have to follow through on the whole procedure until they learn to walk on their own.

Why can't we love the young children of God in the same way? Why can't we overlook their growing pains? People may grumble, "I thought you taught so-and-so God's Word and, look, he's not doing anything. Explain that." I don't have to explain it. The person was a young child spiritually, and it was my responsibility to watch over him. But when he was skidding around, I didn't beat him to death. We nurture the young; we love them and pick them up when they stumble. When a little toddler falls, we don't spank him; we go help pick him up and encourage him. But somehow or other, we think that a Christian should walk like God Almighty from the moment he is born again. How ridiculous! The point is that you never learn to walk until you start walking. If you are afraid of mistakes, you will never grow, because you never exercise. We cannot be servants unless we walk.

> II Corinthians 4:6:
> For God, who commanded the light to shine out of darkness, hath shined in our hearts, to *give* the light of the knowledge of the glory of God in the face of Jesus Christ.

What a tremendous "shining-in." God has shined in our hearts, He has done it, "to give the light of the knowledge." My friends, unless the light of that knowledge is given to others by those of us who have had it shine in our hearts, the light of that knowledge just isn't going to be spread. God's Word isn't going to be heard unless we tell it. And we *can* tell it because we have heard it.

> II Corinthians 4:7:
> But we have this treasure in earthen vessels....

We have this treasure of the knowledge of the glory of God in the face of Jesus Christ; we have this treasure, God's Word, the holy spirit within. To be sons of God and servants to our fellowmen, we have this treasure "in earthen vessels." We know our human frailties, we know our shortcomings, and we know that at times we get weary even though we shouldn't get weary. The earthen vessels may seem

166

weak, but inside is Christ in us the hope of glory.
That is why we must read the latter part of verse 7.

> ...that the excellency of the power [in making
> known the greatness of His Word and power]
> may be of God, and not of us.

Within our own selves there would not be that
strength; but when it is Christ in us, then he is our
strength—he infuses his strength in us. He is the
Word within us; he is the power; he is everything
the Word says he is. And all of that is in us, in earthen
vessels, that the power may be of God.

The signs, miracles and wonders which are coming
to pass around the world are happening because sons
of God are believing God's Word and are telling
His Word as it is purely written, not adulterated.
The people whose eyes are not blinded are seeing
it. The Word promises, "Blessed *are* they which do
hunger and thirst after righteousness: for they shall
be filled." So if you want to be filled, just get hungry
and thirsty. You will be filled according to the degree
of your hunger. Once you have learned a bit of truth
from God's Word, you never need to hunger and
thirst for that truth again. In your continued spiritual
growth you will simply hunger for more and more
truth and knowledge from the Word of God. But
once you have tasted of that food, once you have

167

had a drink of that water of life, at that point you will never need to hunger or thirst again—provided the nourishment is the rightly-divided Word. What a privilege we have to live in this day and to be able to hold forth God's Word. This is the most momentous opportunity God could ever give to anyone. He has given this to us, earthen vessels, simple clay jugs. But on the inside, it is God in Christ in us. What excellency of power!

Part IV

The Greatness of the Church of Grace

Part IV

The Treatment of
Obsolescence

Part IV

The Greatness of the Church of Grace

Only with an accurate understanding of God's Word can we fully appreciate how great and how wonderful the Age of Grace in which we are living truly is. Chapter 10, "The Church" is a primer of basic knowledge for a believer. Its divisions give an index into the breadth of this study: To or for whom are the books of the Bible written, The three doctrinal epistles, The word "mystery," The word "church," The great mystery, The great mystery hid, The Church of the Body terminates, plus two afternotes about man's day and the Lord's Day, and ending with an appendix.

"God's Dwelling Place" explains why God yearned for the coming of the Church of Grace. Ever since the fall of man, God sought a permanent dwelling place in order to have fellowship with His children. He gave Moses instructions to build a tabernacle. He gave Solomon instructions to build the temple in Jerusalem. But these were temporary meeting

The Greatness of the Church of Grace

places for God and His children. God's perfect plan came about on the day of Pentecost when His spirit was placed within each believer. Now He has a permanent dwelling place within each of us and we can commune with God in spirit and in truth.

This book appropriately culminates with "The Final Victory," which is a thrilling look, verse by verse, at I Corinthians 15. God does not want us ignorant concerning the end of time. So this chapter in I Corinthians tells the sequence of events of the last times and thereby gives us great comfort and encouragement to live with all our being for the Lord.

God has given us believers in the Church of Grace so much knowledge and power—in fact, *all* things that pertain to life and godliness. How grateful we are! Let us always abound in the work of the Lord as we look forward to the final victory.

CHAPTER TEN

The Church:
The Great Mystery Revealed
INTRODUCTION

When the great mystery of the Body of Christ was first declared by the Apostle Paul at Ephesus, the record in Acts 19 states, "So mightily grew the Word of God and prevailed," to the end that "all they which dwelt in Asia heard the word of the Lord Jesus, both Jews and Greeks [Gentiles]." Yet some years later, before the close of his life, Paul declared in his second letter to Timothy, "that all they which are in Asia be turned away from me." *II Tim 1:15* When followers of Paul's turned away even before the end of his lifetime, they lost the excitement and the full comprehension of Paul's revelation concerning the mystery. Thus the mystery was really forgotten.

The failure of Paul's followers to adhere to the good news of the great mystery resulted in their turning to error. In II Timothy 2:18, Paul speaks of those "who concerning the truth have erred." In chapter 3, verse 8, he speaks of those who "resist the truth." In chapter 4, verse 4, he speaks of those

171

who "turn away *their* ears from the truth, and shall be turned unto fables."

When the first century believers stopped walking in the light of the great mystery, as the epistle to the Ephesians unfolds it so fully, they lost the power which comes with understanding the mystery which is the center of all true Christian faith, the one Body of Christ.

The immediate consequence of the loss of this truth brought about many erroneous doctrines. It initiated the different so-called "bodies," consequently causing many divisions and schisms within the Church. Instead of rightly dividing the Word of Truth and recognizing the one Body which God made, as disclosed in Ephesians 4:4, men established their own ecclesiastical bodies and sects.

After losing the knowledge of the mystery and the Church of Grace, the next major loss was the truth concerning the believer's perfect standing before God through Christ. The truths that God justifies every believer by the faith of Jesus Christ and that He saves every believer by grace were buried asunder. After failing to understand these truths, unlearned teachers began to propagate error regarding the Lord's promised return from heaven, the gathering together, and the resurrection. Preparation for

172

death and judgment replaced the great hope of the blessed return of Christ. Spiritual darkness engulfed the Christian world, and "religion" (man-made forms of worship) defined most of Christianity. This pervasive spiritual darkness is yet around us and upon us. We Christians have not recaptured the basic truth of the revelation of the great mystery. The first truth to be lost is usually the last to be regained, so it needs to be recovered and taught to people who love God and want to understand the doctrines of His inspired Word. *p / 8 9*

Before the Lord Jesus Christ ascended into heaven, he made the solemn declaration given in John 16:12-15.

> I have yet many things to say unto you, but ye cannot bear them now.
>
> Howbeit when he, the Spirit of truth, is come, he will guide you into all truth: for he shall not speak of himself; but whatsoever he shall hear, *that* shall he speak: and he will shew you things to come.
>
> He shall glorify me: for he shall receive of mine, and shall shew *it* unto you.
>
> All things that the Father hath are mine: there-

173

fore said I, that he shall take of mine, and shall shew *it* unto you.

Every sincere believer must ask himself the question as to when, where, and how this promise of the Lord Jesus Christ was fulfilled. What is meant by "all truth" or, as the Revised Version has it, "all the truth," into which the Holy Spirit was to guide? It certainly could not mean that the Holy Spirit would show one truth to one person and another truth to another person, and that these truths would be so different that Christians would form into splinter groups, each adhering to his special, unharmonious revelation.

The words of Christ's promise "he will guide... he shall speak...he will show you" are definite. So we have only one place to look for the answer, namely, the epistles which are addressed to the Church of the Body. In these seven epistles we have the perfect truth into which the spirit was to guide and lead. These seven epistles contain all the truth Christ could not speak while on earth, for the time had not yet come for this revelation. These Church epistles contain "the things to come" which the Spirit was to give by revelation, which would "glorify" Christ.

174

To or For Whom
Are the Books of the Bible Written?

Much of our modern-day confusion about the Church is brought on by our not knowing that different parts of the Bible are addressed to different groups of people. The Church epistles which are specifically addressed *to* the believers are being grouped together with sections of the Bible which are simply written *for* the believer's learning. There are seven epistles addressed directly to the Church: Romans, Corinthians, Galatians, Ephesians, Philippians, Colossians, and Thessalonians. Yet the four gospels, and especially the Sermon on the Mount, the Apostles' Creed, the Lord's Prayer, and the ten commandments are frequently accepted as being the basic doctrines of Christianity instead of the knowledge revealed in those epistles specifically and directly addressed *to* the Church. Thus, today there is much ignorance among most Christians concerning what Christ accomplished for us. The believers, not knowing their standing in Christ, their completeness and perfection in him, are blown about with every wind of doctrine. Only the understanding and acceptance of the great revelation given in the Church epistles will ever deliver a believer from all the new sects, doctrines, theories, and schools of thought which have led us away from the inspired Biblical doctrine.

The Greatness of the Church of Grace

The seven Church epistles are set in the Bible in the perfection of their spiritual truth. In none of the manuscripts of the New Testament does the order of these seven Church epistles ever vary, although the order of other books in the New Testament does. This phenomenon alone should speak clearly to our spiritual ears.

Three of the Church epistles—Romans, Ephesians, and Thessalonians—are doctrinal in content. These three contain the basic doctrinal teaching to the Church as compared with the other four epistles— Corinthians, Galatians, Philippians, and Colossians.

The order of this revelation in the Word of God is as follows: Romans sets forth the great doctrine and teaching to the Church on how to believe rightly; Corinthians gives reproof to the Church because of its not following the truth of Romans; and then Galatians establishes the correction as to how to return to the right believing of the doctrinal truths of Romans.

This pattern of these first three books to the Church giving doctrine, reproof, and correction is exactly the same for Ephesians, Philippians, and Colossians.

176

The first step of degradation, when the Word of God is wrongly divided, is to practice error. After practicing error for a period of time, people make a doctrine of it; finally doctrinal errors manifest themselves in creeds, rules, and commandments of men.

Thessalonians stands alone in its teaching of doctrine, without epistles following for reproof and correction. Later we shall describe why Thessalonians is the last Church epistle even though it may have been written first, and why it has no companion epistles of reproof and correction.

DOCTRINAL EPISTLES	REPROOF EPISTLES	CORRECTION EPISTLES
How to believe rightly	Point out the practical error resulting from wrong believing, failing to adhere to the revelation in the doctrinal epistles	Correct doctrinal error resulting from wrong practice, failing to adhere to the revelation in the epistles
ROMANS	CORINTHIANS	GALATIANS
EPHESIANS	PHILIPPIANS	COLOSSIANS
THESSALONIANS	no reproof	no correction
	Thessalonians is the consummation, telling about the return of Christ and the gathering together. There is no possibility of wrong practice here because Jesus Christ himself will execute this event.	

Putting together these seven Church epistles, we not only have the "all truth" Jesus Christ said would be given, but we also have all the truth concerning the "mystery of God and of Christ," to manifest a more abundant life and to be more than conquerors in every situation.

The Three Doctrinal Epistles

We will now view the perfect order and divine reason for the three doctrinal epistles: Romans, Ephesians and Thessalonians.

Romans is placed first among the doctrinal epistles because it contains the foundation, the beginning, the starting point, for the "all truth" knowledge which Christ proclaimed he would send after his ascension. In Romans, man is shown to be in utter depravity and totally helpless; but by God's grace through Jesus Christ, the believer is justified from sin. Romans tells that all believers died with Christ, were buried with Christ, arose with Christ, and were made sons and heirs of God. Romans sets forth God's purpose, will, and desire in making every believer what he is and in giving him what he has in Christ.

Where the magnificent eighth chapter of Romans terminates the doctrinal teaching of Romans regarding the believer, the revelation given in the Book of

Ephesians takes up. Ephesians does not start with man's depravity, as does Romans, but with God's purpose and will for every believer. Ephesians declares, in crystal-clear terms, the rights every believer has been given by Christ.

Note that the first chapter of Ephesians declares that "God...hath blessed [past tense] us with all spiritual blessings" (verse 3). God has chosen us in Christ (verse 4). He has made us lovely and accepted (verse 6). In Christ we have redemption and remission from sin according to the riches of His grace (verse 7). All of Christ's works are to the end that we should be to the praise of His glory (verse 12). All believers are to be enlightened so as to know the riches of His glory in the saints (verse 18). All believers are to know what is the exceeding greatness of His power to us who believe (verse 19).

In Romans the believers receive the good news of what the sinner obtains by grace. In Ephesians the believers receive the revelation of what the great mystery is and the "exceeding greatness of His [God's] power to usward who believe." In Romans the sinner is dealt with individually, while in Ephesians the saved sinners, as one Body—the Body of Christ—are "one new man" collectively. In Romans the believer is dead with Christ (6:8) and risen with him (6:11). In Ephesians the believer

179

is *seated* in the heavenlies with Christ (2:6). In Thessalonians the believer is gathered together forever in glory (II Thessalonians 2:1).

The revelation in Thessalonians stands last. It follows the doctrine of Romans and Ephesians because there is nothing else available to the Church after the believers are gathered with Christ Jesus. The culmination or pinnacle of a believer's existence is reached in Thessalonians, for this epistle gives the revelation that the believer shall be caught up to be with the Lord and be as he is in glory. This is the final revelation of the "all truth" which Christ promised would be sent before we ascend as recorded in the Gospel of John.

The Word of God declares in II Timothy 3:16, "All scripture *is* given by inspiration of God [God-breathed], and *is* profitable for doctrine [right believing: Romans, Ephesians, Thessalonians], for reproof [where we are not believing rightly: Corinthians, Philippians], for correction [to bring us back to right believing: Galatians, Colossians] ...." These three (doctrine, reproof, correction) constitute "instruction in righteousness." Furthermore, the revealed order of these epistles in the Bible is revealing. Romans builds toward the knowledge of Ephesians, and Ephesians prepares the believer for the culmination of the Christian's hope, the return of Christ which is stated in Thessalonians.

The Word "Mystery"

The word "mystery" is a transliteration of the Greek word *mustērion*. The Hebrew word *ratz* is *mustērion* in the Septuagint. The Aramaic word is *araza*. The earliest Latin version of the Greek *musterion* in Ephesians 5:32 is translated *sacramentum*.

The word "mystery" means "concealed," "hidden" or "secret." This was also the meaning of the word *sacramentum* in its earliest usage. However, the usage of the word "mystery" has changed through the years and does not carry the impact of its original Biblical usage. The word "mystery" (*mustērion*) in the Bible means something that is kept secret, yet can be understood when revealed. According to Deuteronomy 29:29, "The secret *things belong* unto the Lord our God: but those *things which are* revealed *belong* unto us and to our children for ever."

The word *mustērion* is found 27 times in the New Testament. Three usages are in the gospels, four in the Book of Revelation, and 20 in the Pauline epistles. The "great mystery" is only one of its usages. Not every use of *mustērion* is in a religious context. A mystery may be related to matters in the realm including actions of men which are done in secrecy.

To the Church of God, the born-again believers, the Body of Christ, there is no subject of such significant importance as the great mystery. The time of the great mystery begins with the day of Pentecost and terminates with the gathering together of the believers. This period is referred to as an administration, *oikonomia*.

In governmental organization, from local government to federal, we have different administrations. For instance, we may have a Republican administration or a Democratic administration, or we may speak of an administration of a certain President. So it is in the Bible. Before the end of time, there will have been seven different administrations, the counting beginning with Genesis 1:1 and going to Revelation 21:20. The administration which preceded the day of Pentecost was the administration of Christ's personal presence upon earth. The Bible refers to this period as the Christ Administration or the Kingdom of Heaven.

The Christ Administration officially ended with his ascension. Yet, in practice, people have acted as though the Christ Administration continued on. This has caused gross misunderstanding and the wrong dividing of the Word. If the Church of Grace began on the day of Pentecost, why did so many born-again believers continue abiding by the law for

182

so many years after Pentecost? We are told in Acts 21:20 "how many thousands of Jews there are which believe; and they are all zealous of the law." What is the answer? It is very simple. Believers were born again on the day of Pentecost and as such were part of the Body of Christ. But since the significance of what came on the day of Pentecost had not been revealed at that time, they, as born-again believers, continued to be zealous for the law. They needed more doctrine to be revealed.

We utilize electricity day in and day out, but we nonscientists cannot explain what it is. So it was on the day of Pentecost when the power from on high was given. Believers were born again, filled with the holy spirit for the first time, but they could not explain what they had received and were operating. They utilized it, they operated it, but they could not define it or describe it, because the explanation of what they had received at Pentecost and thereafter was not given until some time later to the Apostle Paul. This revelation unveiled the great mystery.

The Word "Church"

Before we proceed further in our understanding of the great mystery, we must understand the usage of the word "church" in both the Christ Administration and in the Grace Administration, the latter

183

being the administration in which we all are now living. In the Christ Administration, the Church is called the bride of Christ; in the Grace Administration, the Church is called the Body of Christ. Confusing these two usages and not associating them with the proper and distinct administration has caused no small amount of error.

The Greek word for "church" is *ekklēsia*, literally meaning the "called out." In the Septuagint translation of the Old Testament, the Greek word *ekklēsia* is used 75 times, meaning "to call together for an assembly or for a meeting." *Ekklēsia* is used of any group called together for any specific purpose.

The Greek word *ekklēsia* is the Hebrew word *cahal*. The word *cahal* occurs in the Old Testament 123 times. There it is translated "congregation" 86 times, "assembly" 17 times, "company" 17 times and "multitude" 3 times.

The first usage of *cahal* is given in Genesis 28:3: "That thou mayest be a multitude [*cahal*] of people," namely, they were a called-out people. This is exactly what Israel was: a people called out from among others and assembled together apart from others.

184

Any assembly, any group meeting, called out for a specific purpose is an *ekklēsia*. If you were called out for a meeting, that assembly would be an *ekklēsia*. If a mob were called out to destroy a whole community, this mob would be called an *ekklēsia*. A "union" meeting which ended in mob violence in the Bible is called an *ekklēsia*. Look at Acts 19.

Acts 19:21-32:

After these things were ended, Paul purposed in the spirit, when he had passed through Macedonia and Achaia, to go to Jerusalem, saying, After I have been there, I must also see Rome. So he sent into Macedonia two of them that ministered unto him, Timotheus and Erastus; but he himself stayed in Asia for a season. And the same time there arose no small stir about that way.

For a certain *man* named Demetrius, a silversmith, which made silver shrines for Diana, brought no small gain unto the craftsmen; Whom he called together with the workmen of like occupation, and said, Sirs, ye know that by this craft we have our wealth.

Moreover ye see and hear, that not alone at Ephesus, but almost throughout all Asia, this Paul hath persuaded and turned away much people, saying that they be no gods, which are made with hands: [Watch this *ekklēsia* develop.

185

Demetrius is a real organizer.]
So that not only this our craft is in danger to be
set at nought; but also that the temple of the
great goddess Diana should be despised, and her
magnificence should be destroyed, whom all
Asia and the world worshippeth. [Look at that
build-up. He's got something going here.]
And when they heard *these sayings*, they were
full of wrath, and cried out, saying, Great *is*
Diana of the Ephesians.
And the whole city was filled with confusion:
and having caught Gaius and Aristarchus, men
of Macedonia, Paul's companions in travel,
they rushed with one accord into the theatre.
And when Paul would have entered in unto the
people, the disciples suffered him not [to enter
in].
And certain of the chief of Asia, which were his
friends, sent unto him, desiring *him* that he
would not adventure himself into the theatre.
Some [of the silversmith craftsmen] therefore
cried one thing, and some another: for the
assembly [*ekklēsia*, church] was confused....

Demetrius and his fellow silversmiths were not
called together to worship the true God. They were
called out, assembled by Demetrius, in the interest
of their "union" to maintain their profits as silversmiths of the statues of Diana. The meaning and

186

usage of the word *ekklēsia* is certainly clear from this
Biblical illustration.

Modern usage of the word "church" also varies
depending on the situation. For instance, if you were
pointing out a building you would say, "Look at that
church." This definition of the word "church" is
different from your saying, "We are having a meeting
of the church." Today we also speak of the church
by referring to different denominations such as the
Methodist Church, the Roman Catholic Church, the
Lutheran Church, the Baptist Church. These different usages of the word "church" are understood.
In the Bible also we must rightly divide the usages
of *ekklēsia* and understand the significant meaning
of each usage in the context of the administration
in which it is used.

The *ekklēsia* of the Church of the Gospels which
Jesus Christ initiated is the called out from Israel.
According to Romans 15:8, Jesus Christ was a
minister to the circumcision. Jesus Christ kept and
fulfilled every law given to Israel. Not only did
Jesus Christ come to Israel, but even when he sent
out the twelve apostles, according to Matthew 10,
he sent them only to the lost sheep of the house of
Israel. When the seventy in Luke 10 were commis-
sioned, they were sent to Israel only. Jesus' entire
ministry was to Israel, the circumcision. Jesus

187

Christ's message was a calling out of followers from Israel.

Matthew 16:18 contains a statement which is usually misconstrued, where Jesus said, "And I say also unto thee, That thou art Peter, and upon this rock I will build my church [*ekklēsia*]."

The word "Peter" is the Greek word *petros*, meaning "the small grain-like substance of sand." Every time the wind blows, the tiny grain blows. The Greek word for "rock" is *petra*, meaning "a solid mass of unmovable stone." This scripture does not declare that the Church of the Gospel is built upon Peter. On the contrary, it speaks loudly saying, "You are Peter [*petros*, a grain of sand; you, Peter, blow around with everything], but upon this rock [*petra*, a solid mass of stone, which is Christ], I will build my church." The Church in the Gospels was built by Jesus Christ himself, who was the bridegroom, and the "called out" are the bride.

The Church of the bride, the called out of Israel, temporarily terminated with the death of the bridegroom. More accurately, the Church of the bride is being held in abeyance until the period or the administration of grace has culminated. Jesus Christ as the bridegroom takes up again beginning with the Revelation Administration. Jesus Christ will then be the

188

King of kings and the bridegroom. At that time he will build the Church from the called out of Israel against which the gates of hell shall not prevail. The Gospels terminate with the suffering Christ, and the Book of Revelation contains the glory of Christ.

The Church as the bride of Christ was no mystery. Israel's blessings, as well as the blessings on the Gentiles through Israel and the coming and the works of the Messiah, were no secrets. See Genesis 12:3; 18:18; 22:18; 28:14; Psalms 27:1; Isaiah 49:6; Luke 2:30-32.

The sufferings and glory of Christ were no secret. The Old Testament prophets were totally conversant with the truth of "the sufferings of Christ, and the glory that should follow," as I Peter 1:11 tells. But everyone was baffled by an unexplained period of time between the "sufferings and the glory." Thus they searched diligently to find it.

The Great Mystery

I Peter 1:10-12 is the basis of truth from which we launch into the detailed study and understanding of the great mystery.

189

I Peter 1:10:
Of which salvation the prophets have inquired
and searched diligently, who prophesied of the
grace *that should come* unto you.

These were the Old Testament prophets who saw a
period of time between the "sufferings of Christ, and
the glory that should follow." They searched diligently in the Word for the meaning and duration of
that period, but their efforts proved fruitless as that
period was known only to God Himself.

I Peter 1:11 and 12:
Searching what, or what manner of time the
Spirit of Christ which was in them did signify,
when it testified beforehand the sufferings of
Christ, and the glory that should follow.
Unto whom [the Old Testament prophets] it
was revealed, that not unto themselves, but unto
us they did minister the things, which are now
reported unto you by them [the Church apostles
and prophets in Ephesians 4:11] that have
preached the gospel unto you with the Holy
Ghost sent down from heaven; which things the
angels desire to look into.

190

The Old Testament prophets searched for the length of time of the Grace Period, between the sufferings of Christ and the glory that should follow. There were prophecies of Christ's coming throughout the Old Testament, as well as the details of his sufferings and glory. But for occurrences of the time between the sufferings and the glory, the prophets of old unfruitfully searched the Scriptures. They could not find what was to happen for they sought the period of the great mystery.

Even the angels did not know the duration of the period of time between the sufferings and the glory of Christ. This period is the great *mustērion*, which was according to Ephesians 3:9 "hid in God," "hid from ages and from generations" (Colossians 1:26); "kept secret since the world began," in Romans 16:25; never made known "in other ages," in Ephesians 3:5. Not a single word was written or heard of this great mystery until it was revealed in detail to the Apostle Paul.

Note carefully what Ephesians 3 says about this mystery.

> Ephesians 3:2-9:
> If ye have heard of the dispensation [administration] of the grace of God which is given me to you-ward:

191

How that by revelation he made known unto me the mystery; (as I wrote afore in few words.
Whereby, when ye read, ye may understand my knowledge in the mystery of Christ)
Which in other ages was not made known unto the sons of men, as it is now revealed unto his holy apostles and prophets by the Spirit;
That the Gentiles should be fellowheirs, and of the same body, and partakers of his promise in Christ by the gospel:
Whereof I was made a minister, according to the gift of the grace of God given unto me by the effectual working of his power.
Unto me, who am less than the least of all saints, is this grace given, that I should preach among the Gentiles the unsearchable riches of Christ;
And to make all *men* see what *is* the fellowship [*oikonomia*, administration] of the mystery [*musterion*], which from the beginning of the world hath been hid in God, who created all things by Jesus Christ.

The Epistle to the Colossians also speaks of the mystery.

Colossians 1:24-27:
...For his body's sake, which is the church: Whereof I am made a minister, according to the

dispensation [administration] of God which is
given to me for you, to fulfill the word of God;
Even the mystery which hath been hid from ages
and from generations, but now is made manifest
to his saints:
To whom God would make known what *is* the
riches of the glory of this mystery [*mustērion*],
among the Gentiles; which is Christ in you, the
hope of glory.

Romans 16 has this illuminating truth regarding
the mystery.

Romans 16:25 and 26:
Now to him that is of power to stablish you
according to my gospel, and the preaching of
Jesus Christ, according to the revelation of the
mystery [*mustērion*], which was kept secret
since the world began.
But now is made manifest, and by the scriptures
of the prophets, according to the commandment
of the everlasting God, made known to all nations for the obedience of faith.

In all the relevant scriptures of Ephesians, Colossians and Romans, we note one repeated truth: the
mystery regarding the Church, the Body of Christ,
had never before been made known until it was
revealed to the Apostle Paul. The mystery "in other

193

ages was not made known"; "hid from ages and from generations"; "kept secret since the world began"; "hid in God" from the beginning. Therefore, that mystery cannot be revealed in the Old Testament or in the gospels, for then it would not have been a mystery. Once a truth is revealed it is no longer a mystery.

The Great Mystery: What It Is

The great mystery was that the "Gentiles should be fellowheirs, and of the same body" (Ephesians 3:6), and that it is "Christ in you" which is "the riches of the glory of this mystery" (Colossians 1:27). This is the Church, the called out from both Jew and Gentile, making one new man, a new body in Him.

Ephesians 2:11-16:
Wherefore remember, that ye *being* in time past Gentiles in the flesh, who are called Uncircumcision by that which is called the Circumcision in the flesh made by hands;
That at that time ye were without Christ, being aliens from the commonwealth of Israel, and strangers from the covenants of promise, having no hope, and without God in the world:
But now in Christ Jesus ye who sometimes were

far off are made nigh by the blood of Christ.
For he is our peace, who hath made both one,
and hath broken down the middle wall of
partition *between us*;
Having abolished in his flesh the enmity, *even*
the law of commandments *contained* in ordinances; for to make in himself of twain one new
man, *so* making peace;
And that he might reconcile both unto God in
one body by the cross, having slain the enmity
thereby.

The Church as the bride in the gospels has the
bridegroom, Christ, who will build his Church,
according to Matthew 16:18. The Church as the
Body is not composed of two, like the bride and
bridegroom, but is one new man, one body, of which
Christ is the head. In this Church of the Body, the
work of reconciling men and women to God is not
the work of Christ, but the work of the believers who
have been given the word and the ministry of reconciliation.

II Corinthians 5:18-20:
And all things *are* of God, who hath reconciled
us to himself by Jesus Christ, and hath given to
us the ministry of reconciliation;
To wit, that God was in Christ, reconciling the
world unto himself, not imputing their tres-

passes unto them; and hath committed unto us the word of reconciliation.

Now then we are ambassadors for Christ, as though God did beseech *you* by us: we pray *you* in Christ's stead, be ye reconciled to God.

The Church of the bride is built by the bridegroom; the Church of the Body of Christ continues to grow because of the work of born-again believers.

The Great Mystery Hid

Why was the great mystery kept secret for so long a period of time after Pentecost?

I Corinthians 2:1 and 2:

And I, brethren, when I came to you, came not with excellency of speech or of wisdom, declaring unto you the testimony [mystery, *mustēri-ion*] of God.

For I determined not to know any thing among you, save Jesus Christ, and him crucified.

Why could Paul tell some in the Corinthian church only about Jesus Christ and him crucified? Because the majority of believers were not spiritually mature enough to accept more truth. They could not be taught the mystery. This is a tremendous truth. The Church of the Body is not made alive because of

Jesus Christ's crucifixion; we are alive because of his
resurrection and the new birth that became available
on the day of Pentecost. Yet, most people today do
not spiritually go beyond Jesus Christ and his crucifixion. The center or focal point of almost every
church is the altar and the cross.

I Corinthians 2:6:
Howbeit [however] we speak wisdom among
them that are perfect: yet not the wisdom of
this world, nor of the princes of this world, that
come to nought.

The word "perfect," *teleios* is the key. Among the
Christian believers was a small handful of *teleioi*,
mature, spiritually grown-up believers as opposed to
babes in Christ or carnal Christians. To those few
teleioi, "initiated ones," Paul could speak the wisdom
of God regarding the great mystery [*mustērion*]
"even the hidden *wisdom*, which God ordained before the world unto our glory."

I Corinthians 2:7 and 8:
But we speak the wisdom of God in a mystery,
even the hidden *wisdom*, which God ordained
before the world unto our glory:
Which none of the princes of this world knew:
for had they known *it*, they would not have
crucified the Lord of glory.

197

This was the great mystery, "which none of the princes of this world knew." The prince of this world is Satan. Had he and his chief devil spirits known the great mystery "they would not have crucified the Lord of glory." Satan would have preferred a living Jesus Christ in one place at a time rather than Christ Jesus living in every born-again believer. Every born-again believer has Christ in him and is capable of doing the work that Christ did; besides, believers can lead others into the new birth, a thing which Christ himself did not do while on earth, for the new birth was not available until Pentecost. Jesus Christ's ministry on earth was necessary in order to prepare the way for the new birth. In addition, God's resurrecting Christ from the grave was required, plus Christ's ministry for forty days after the resurrection, and the eight days after the ascension, to bring to pass the reality of the new birth and the great mystery. Because God did not want Satan to know His plan, the great *mustērion* was "hid in God from before the foundations of the world" and did not become a reality in any believer's life until the day of Pentecost.

While Jesus Christ was personally present upon the earth, he could be at only one place at one time. Since the day of Pentecost, Christ is present wherever there is a born-again believer. Since the day of Pentecost, the Church is the Body, with Christ in each believer. The bride and bridegroom are two, but Christ in you makes every believer a member of the one Body. The early Church was cognizant of this great reality and they did signs, miracles, and wonders.

Christ, who is in heaven, is the head of the Church, the Body. Christ's people are members of his Body. The born-again believers are "all members of that body," not on earth but in Christ, the head, who is in heaven. The unity and oneness of the Body of the Church springs not from the "eye or hand" members, but from the source, the head, Christ Jesus. I Corinthians 12:18 says, "But now hath God set the members . . . in the body [in Christ in heaven], as it hath pleased him [God]," not as it seems to have pleased men.

The members of the Body of Christ are those who have been born again by confessing not their sins but the savior from sin, the Lord Jesus Christ, and believing in their hearts that God raised Jesus Christ from the dead, as stated in Romans 10:9. This great salvation is in Jesus Christ the savior, in whom the members of the Body were circumcised when he was circumcised; baptized when he was baptized; fulfilled all the law when he fulfilled it and said "IT is finished"; died when he died; were buried when he was buried; rose again when he arose; ascended when he ascended; and (as members of the Body, the Church, the called out) are "seated in the heavenlies"; "complete in him"; rejoicing in the truth that the members shall "never more come into condemnation"; have escaped the "wrath of God"; have "passed from death unto life"; and are looking forward to that day when the earthly part of that Body will be "received up into glory."

The growth of this Body, the Church, comes from the head, Christ Jesus, who is in heaven. God exalted Jesus Christ by the resurrection from the dead and, as set forth in Ephesians 1:22 and 23, "gave him *to be* the head over all *things* to the church, Which is his body, the fulness of him that filleth all in all." The head, Christ Jesus, is the one who fills all the members of his Body with all that God gives in the new birth, which is Christ in you the hope of glory. As the head of the natural body coordinates or guides the natural body, so the head of the spiritual Body is spiritually the source of guidance for the whole spiritual Body which is the Church.

According to a literal translation of Ephesians 4:15 and 16, God wants the Body of Christ to become a perfect man that all the members upon earth "may grow up into him in all things, which is the head, even Christ: From whom the whole Body fitly joined together and compacted by every sensation from the

200

supply, according to a working, corresponding to the measure of each individual part, brings about the growth of the Body with a view to the building up of itself in love."

To grow to perfect man requires the operation of the gift ministries listed in Ephesians 4:11.

> And he [Christ] gave some, apostles; and some, prophets; and some, evangelists; and some, pastors and teachers.

The specific purpose for having these ministries is given in verses 12 and 13.

> For the perfecting of the saints, for [with a view to] the work of the ministry, for [with a further view to] the edifying of the body of Christ: Till [until] we all come in the unity [oneness] of the faith, and of the knowledge of the Son of God, unto a perfect man, unto the measure of the stature of the fulness of Christ.

The outcome of the gift ministries is given in verses 14, 15 and 16 of Ephesians 4:

> That we *henceforth* be no more children, tossed to and fro, and carried about with every wind of doctrine, by the sleight of men, *and* cunning

201

craftiness, whereby they lie in wait to deceive; But speaking the truth in love, may grow up into him in all things, which is the head, *even* Christ: From whom the whole body fitly joined together and compacted by that which every joint supplieth, according to the effectual working in the measure of every part, maketh increase of the body unto the edifying of itself in love.

The growth of the Church is God downward, not man upward. Colossians 2:19 says it is from heaven to earth and not a reaching up from earth to heaven. The origin of the Body, the Church, is God who hath given Christ to be head over all things to this wondrous Body. Christ, the head, is the source of all guidance and operation of the Body. The members of this Body of Christ are to work in the Body in the relationship that God has set, and not according to what men have set. Natural, earthly, carnal rules, regulations and ordinances do not enter into the growth of this Body of Christ at all, for this Body is totally spiritual, heavenly and eternal.

Paul's instruction to Timothy, his "own son in the faith," regarding the continuation of the ministry in Ephesus after Paul moved on to Macedonia, is filled with enlightenment regarding the teaching of the great mystery. Paul instructs Timothy in I Timothy

1:3 to "charge some that they teach no other doctrine." Timothy is told to inform people that there is no other way of right believing than the truth of the great mystery. Furthermore, Timothy is not to allow them to "give heed to fables," that is, "I think this" or "I think that." Also Timothy is not to give heed to "endless genealogies," where one group, like a family, would say, "We are much older than you, therefore we know more," or "We have been conducting this family fellowship a long time; we may teach for right believing what we want to." Paul specifically instructs Timothy not to permit this to occur. All this talk of family philosophy will engender nothing but questions and doubts. This foolishness will not promote "godly edifying" [*oikonomia*], which is the "administration of God," the mystery, which is by "the faith of Jesus Christ."

In I Timothy 1:11 the great mystery is referred to as "the glorious gospel of the blessed God" or, more accurately, as "the gospel of the glory of God."

In I Timothy 3:9 the great secret is called "the mystery of the faith" which is to be held in a sound conscience.

203

The Church of the Body Terminates

The administration of the great mystery, the Age of Grace, the Church as the Body of Christ, will be concluded when I Thessalonians 4:13-18 has come to pass.

> But I would not have you to be ignorant, brethren, concerning them which are asleep, that ye sorrow not, even as others which have no hope.
>
> For if we believe that Jesus died and rose again even so them also which sleep in Jesus will God bring with him.
>
> For this we say unto you by the word of the Lord, that we which are alive *and* remain unto the coming of the Lord shall not prevent [precede] them which are asleep.
>
> For the Lord himself shall descend from heaven with a shout, with the voice of the archangel, and with the trump of God: and the dead in Christ shall rise first:
>
> Then we which are alive *and* remain shall be caught up [away] together with them in the clouds, to meet the Lord in the air: and so [in this manner] shall we ever be with the Lord. Wherefore comfort one another with these words.

Christ's return for the Church, the Body of Christ, is not a resurrection. To have a resurrection according to Biblical usage, all must be dead. But, in this Church Age, the period of the great mystery and of grace, not *all* will have died at the time of his return. Therefore, the scripture verse declares that the dead in Christ shall rise and the alive believers at his return shall be changed. This is not a resurrection. In I Corinthians 15, the dead in Christ are called "corruptibles," and the living believers are called "mortals."

After the mortals have put on immortality and the corruptibles have put on incorruption at the gathering together, then is the Administration of the Body of Christ over.

> I Corinthians 15:51-54:
> Behold, I shew you a mystery; We shall not all sleep, but we shall all be changed,
> In a moment, in the twinkling of an eye, at the last trump: for the trumpet shall sound, and the dead shall be raised incorruptible, and we shall be changed.
> For this corruptible must put on incorruption, and this mortal *must* put on immortality.
> So when this corruptible shall have put on incorruption, and this mortal shall have put on immortality, then shall be brought to pass the

saying that is written, Death is swallowed up in victory.

After the Church as the Body is gathered together unto Christ, the Period or the Administration of Revelation begins.

Man's Day: Present

Confusing the Church of the Body, whose dead in Christ shall rise and the alive shall be changed, with the resurrection of the Church of the bride of Christ has caused untold problems. The teaching that the Church of the Body goes through the tribulation is built on confusing the usage of the word "resurrection" with the "gathering together."

The Church as the Body will have been gathered together by Christ before the "great and notable day of the Lord comes to pass," which is the "day of wrath," also called "the Lord's Day," a part of which is "the first resurrection."

Today in this Age of Grace, the great mystery administration, it is man who does the judging and therefore it is called "man's day," as distinct from "the Lord's Day."

206

I Corinthians 4:3:
But with me it is a very small thing that I
should be judged of you, or of man's judgment.

The word "judgment" is the word "day." Man
does the judging now because this is man's day. But,
there is a day coming when God will do the judging,
and that period is called the "day of Christ" which
includes the Lord's Day. The Lord's Day is the Book
of Revelation period when Christ comes as King of
kings and Lord of lords.

The King James Version's translation of II Thessalonians 2:3 has caused some to believe that the
Church of Grace will go through the tribulation period. The misunderstanding involves the phrase "except there come a falling away first." Let's look
closely at II Thessalonians 2.

Verse 1:
Now we beseech you, brethren, by the coming
of our Lord Jesus Christ, and *by* our gathering
together unto him.

Verse 2:
That ye be not soon shaken in mind, or be
troubled, neither by spirit, nor by word, nor by
letter as from us, as that the day of Christ is at
hand.

207

Verse 3:
Let no man deceive you by any means: for *that day shall not come*, except there come a falling away first, and that man of sin be revealed, the son of perdition.

If the "day of Christ" of verse 2 and "our gathering together unto him" of verse 1, do not occur until after there has been a "falling away and that man of sin be revealed," then the tribulation spoken of in Revelation will indeed be upon us, the Church of the Body. But if the period of wrath of the Book of Revelation is to be endured by the born-again believers, then Christ lived, died, and rose in vain and Pentecost is meaningless and Christianity is senseless. Then, too, the Word of God given for our comfort (I Thessalonians 4:18) becomes our anxious concern. However, that is not the case.

The Geneva Bible and the Cranmer Bible, first published in 1537, and the Tyndale Bible, published in 1539, all predating the King James Version, translate "a falling away first" as "a departure first."

Before the "day of the Lord," there must be a departure of the born-again believers from this world to be with Christ. After the believers have departed with Christ, then will come to pass the revealing of the "man of sin" which will be followed by "the day of wrath."

In II Thessalonians 2:3 the Greek words for "a falling away" are *he apostasia*. The word *he* is the article "the." The prefix *apo* means "away from." Having a circle, *apo* would be illustrated as a line in motion from the exterior of the circle to some distant point. *Stasia* means "to separate," or "draw out." *He apostasia* is "the separation away from" or "the drawing out from among;" it is a departure.

Here is an accurate translation of II Thessalonians 2:3: "Let no man deceive you by any means; for *that day shall not* come, except there be a departure first, and that man of sin be revealed, the son of perdition." How satisfying it is to know that II Thessalonians 2:3 really says that the coming of our Lord Jesus Christ and the born-again believers' "gathering together unto him" will have become a reality before the "day of Christ" is at hand upon the earth. For the "day of Christ" cannot come upon the earth until after the departure.

Lord's Day: Future

Revelation 20:5 pertains to the "Lord's Day" which refers to the Church of the bride and bridegroom period, not the Church of the Body which by that time will have been gathered together.

But the rest of the dead lived not again until the thousand years were finished. This *is* the first resurrection.

There will be a marked contrast between man's day now and the Lord's Day. Isaiah 61 contrasted with Luke 4 gives an indication of this difference. Jesus quotes part of Isaiah 61 in his first recorded message in a synagogue in Nazareth.

Luke 4:16-21:
And he came to Nazareth, where he had been brought up: and, as his custom was, he went into the synagogue on the sabbath day, and stood up for to read. [In reverence and respect for the Word of God, the priest would stand while reading from the scrolls and sit down while teaching.]
And there was delivered unto him the book [scroll] of the prophet Esaias [Isaiah]. And when he had opened the book, he found the place where it was written,
The Spirit of the Lord *is* upon me, because he hath anointed me to preach the gospel to the poor; he hath sent me to heal the brokenhearted, to preach deliverance to the captives, and recovering of sight to the blind, to set at liberty them that are bruised,
To preach the acceptable year of the Lord.

210

And he closed the book, and he gave *it* again to the minister, and sat down. And the eyes of all them that were in the synagogue were fastened on him.

And he began to say unto them, This day is this scripture fulfilled in your ears.

Reading from the scroll of Isaiah, corresponding to our Isaiah 61:1 and 2, Jesus Christ read only to the words "acceptable year of the Lord"; then he closed the scroll and said, "This day is this scripture fulfilled in your ears."

Jesus Christ did not continue to read the "day of vengeance of our God" from Isaiah 61:2, for then he could not have said, "This day is this scripture fulfilled." The "day of vengeance of our God" is still in the future, starting with the Book of Revelation period. There are already almost two thousand years of the Period of Grace history, the great mystery administration, represented by that little comma between the word "Lord" and "and" in Isaiah 61:2. Between "the acceptable year of our Lord" which was then, and "the day of vengeance of our God" which is future, is the administration of the great mystery. The Church as the Body of Christ is awaiting his return to be gathered together unto Christ Jesus who is the head over all.

CHAPTER ELEVEN

God's Dwelling Place

Ever since the fall of Adam, at which time man lost God's created spirit,* God throughout the many centuries sought a permanent dwelling place. In Old Testament times, God gave instructions to Moses for building a tabernacle. Later on He directed Solomon to construct the temple. But none of those abodes was satisfactory. They were only temporary types of dwellings or meeting places for God and His children.

Throughout the centuries God awaited the Age of Grace, which began on the day of Pentecost. It was from this great day on that God could create spirit within man, those people who were His followers.

---

*According to John 4:24, God is Spirit. The Word of God teaches that God originally made man as a threefold being, having a spirit [the quality of which God is constituted], but also a body and a soul. God was with Adam by way of the spirit He had created in him. Man had spirit in common with God. And it was the spirit within man that enabled man to communicate with God and God to communicate with man. It gave them fellowship.

Most of the knowledge of this greatness of the occurrence of Pentecost was lost shortly after the death of the Apostle Paul. Christians didn't lose the spirit which was a gift from God, but they didn't crystallize the truth of God's revelation to the end that they really understood and believed the fullness of it in their hearts. That is still frequently the case today, even among so-called knowledgeable Christians. We never get a great enough vision of the significance of that dwelling place of God which—on Pentecost and ever since—is within every believer.

Isaiah 57 demonstrates the vastness of God and describes His habitation.

> Isaiah 57:15:
> For thus saith the high and lofty One [God] that [who] inhabiteth eternity, whose name *is* Holy; I dwell in the high and holy *place*, with him also *that is* of a contrite and humble spirit, to revive the spirit of the humble, and to revive the heart of the contrite ones.

"For thus saith the high and lofty One [speaking of God] that [who] inhabiteth eternity...." This shows that even heaven is not great enough for God. He also inhabits eternity. This is substantiated by the Book of Kings.

214

I Kings 8:27:
But will God indeed dwell on the earth? behold,
the heaven and heaven of heavens cannot contain thee....

Though these scriptures tell of the vastness of God,
one still wonders where God chose to communicate
with His people. To search out this answer, let's
begin with Psalms 27.

Psalms 27:4 and 5:
One *thing* have I desired of the Lord, that will
I seek after; that I may dwell in the house of
the Lord all the days of my life, to behold
the beauty of the Lord, and to inquire in his
temple [find out about Him].
For in the time of trouble he shall hide me in
his pavilion: in the secret of his tabernacle
shall he hide me; he shall set me up upon a
rock.

Thus the temple was a place to gain knowledge and
love of God, as well as a refuge from troubles. God
dwelt in the tabernacle and the temple, during the
Age of Law; but sometime after the ending of the
law on Pentecost, Stephen, speaking by revelation,
summarized these former meeting places.

Acts 7:37-50:

This is that Moses, which said unto the children of Israel, A prophet [Jesus Christ] shall the Lord your God raise up unto you of your brethren, like unto me [Moses]; him shall ye hear.

This is he, that was in the church in the wilderness with the angel which spake to him in the mount Sina, and *with* our fathers: who received the lively [living] oracles to give unto us:

To whom our fathers would not obey, but thrust *him* from them, and in their hearts turned back again into Egypt,

Saying unto Aaron, Make us gods to go before us: for *as for* this Moses, which [who] brought us out of the land of Egypt, we wot [know] not what is become of him.

And they made a calf in those days, and offered sacrifice unto the idol, and rejoiced in the works of their own hands.

Then God turned, and gave them up to worship the host of heaven; as it is written in the book of the prophets, O ye house of Israel, have ye offered to me slain beasts and sacrifices *by the space of* forty years in the wilderness?

Yea, ye took up the tabernacle of Moloch, and the star of your god Remphan, figures which ye made to worship them: and I will carry you away beyond Babylon.

Our fathers had the tabernacle of witness in
the wilderness, as he had appointed, speaking
unto Moses, that he should make it according
to the fashion that he had seen [which God
gave him by revelation].
Which also our fathers that came after brought
in with Jesus [Joshua] into the possession of the
Gentiles, whom God drave out before the face
of our fathers, unto the days of David;
Who found favour before God, and desired to
find a tabernacle for the God of Jacob [Israel].
But Solomon built him an house.
Howbeit the most High dwelleth not in temples
made with hands; as saith the prophet,
Heaven *is* my throne, and earth *is* my footstool:
what house will ye build me? saith the Lord:
or what *is* the place of my rest?
Hath not my hand made all these things?

Throughout the centuries, God has always revealed
as much of Himself as people were capable of perceiv-
ing. Because Israel could not remain faithful to their
leader, the Prophet Moses, and to the revelation that
God showed him, God gave His children an added,
tangible sign of His presence by having Moses build
a tabernacle. After that, God dealt with David and
then had Solomon build the temple. Again, this was
a witness of God's doing His best for His people.

God was always seeking a dwelling place, a place where He would be reverenced, respected, obeyed. It was to be a place where He would have man's undivided, absolute worship. But a temple was not big enough for God's extensiveness. God who inhabits eternity, needs both heaven and earth and even eternity, thus Moses' tabernacle and Solomon's temple were not truly satisfactory. These structures were only provisional arrangements. They were temporary measures until God could bring about in due time a permanent, perfect dwelling place.

It is important in proceeding toward an understanding of God's finding a permanent habitation that we note the three different parts of the temple and their significance. One part of the temple was made up of the sacred courts and the colonnades. Another part included the court of the Gentiles, that court where the moneychangers were seated when Jesus came in and overthrew the tables and drove out the animals. The third was the innermost part of the temple, the Holy of Holies. A wall separated these various sections of the temple. On the day of Jesus' crucifixion, the veil was destroyed between the court of the Gentiles and the Jews. But more important, the wall or veil between the Jews and the Holy of Holies was also destroyed. Ephesians 2 tells part of the story.

218

Ephesians 2:14:

For he [Jesus Christ] is our peace, who hath made both [Jew and Gentile] one, and hath broken down [destroyed] the middle wall of partition *between us* [between Jew and Gentile]

Jesus Christ brought peace in tearing down the partition separating Jew from Gentile. God no longer held one person or group of persons in higher esteem than any other. As Peter observed, much to his amazement, at Cornelius' house, as recorded in Acts 10:34, "Of a truth I perceive that God is no respecter of persons." Jesus Christ had caused all people, Gentile and Jew, to be equal before God.

The temple had a wall separating the Gentiles from the court of Israel and another wall separating the court of Israel from the Holy of Holies thus signifying the preferred treatment of high priests from the rest of the body of Jews. Covering that entrance into the Holy of Holies was the veil which was torn from top to bottom on the day of the crucifixion.

Mark 15:38:

And the veil of the temple was rent in twain from the top to the bottom.

By his sacrifice, Jesus Christ brought about the tearing of the veil between the court of Israel and the

Holy of Holies, and he also utterly destroyed the temple's separation between Gentiles and Jews. What did Jesus Christ accomplish in ending these separations? He brought peace with God. There would no longer be discrimination between Jew and Gentile. Jesus Christ put them on an equal footing in God's sight.

> Ephesians 2:15:
> [Jesus Christ] Having abolished in his flesh the enmity, *even* the law of commandments *contained* in ordinances; for to make [create] in himself of twain one new man, *so* making peace.

"Having abolished in his flesh the enmity..." means that Jesus Christ totally destroyed the inability of man to know God personally. To state it in the positive, Jesus Christ made it possible for man to know God personally. Jesus Christ abolished in his flesh the enmity and the law of commandments. The enmity specifically relates to the natural men of body and soul who were basically the Gentiles. The law of commandments contained in ordinances was given to Israel, the Jews. Thus when Jesus Christ abolished the enmity for the Gentiles and the law of commandments for the Jews, he tore down the obstacles which were separating each group from God and then he created of twain, from these two types, one new man.

220

Jesus Christ took the Jew and Gentile and broke down the partitions separating them "...so making peace." Why did Jesus Christ abolish the enmity and the ordinances? This was all done in order that God might create one new man. The word "create" is absolutely accurate. That creation is the spirit. What Jesus Christ brought about was the new creation of God in Christ in every believer, regardless of their previous label as Jew or Gentile. There were no longer the two classifications, but a new creation in Christ Jesus.

Ephesians 2:16:
And that he might reconcile [bring back together that which has been separated] both [Jew and Gentile] unto God in one body by the cross, having slain the enmity thereby.

Israel was never able to keep the law, so they were without God. The Gentiles were also without God. So Jesus Christ had to reconcile both types "unto God in one body by the cross, having slain the enmity thereby." So the Gentiles were not only enmity to God, but Israel also, who couldn't keep the law of commandments, was enmity to Him. Jesus Christ needed to reconcile both to God.

221

Ephesians 2:17:
And [Jesus Christ] came and preached peace to you which were afar off, and to them that were nigh.

There are several kinds of preaching in the Bible, but this preaching of Ephesians 2:17 is the good news of the destruction of the enmity and the commandments and of Christ's making peace and reconciling Jew and Gentile to God in one body. The good news came "...to you which were afar off [Gentiles], and to them that were nigh [Israel]." Israel had had God's goodness constantly available to them, so they should have been grateful. But they weren't. Moreover, both groups needed Jesus Christ, the Messiah, and his saving grace.

Ephesians 2:18:
For through him [Jesus Christ] we both have access by one Spirit unto *[pros]* the Father.

There is only one God to whom both Jews and Gentiles have to be reconciled. Once the reconciliation was accomplished, He became Father to both. When Christ's accomplishments were complete, God could then have a permanent dwelling place, not in a temple made with human hands, but in a temple made by His own work. And this temple was His very own children.

The greatness of this fatherly relationship continues to unfold in the next few verses of Ephesians 2 by the usage of certain words whose Greek root is *oikos,* meaning "house," "household" or "family."

> Ephesians 2:19:
> Now therefore [since we have a Father] ye are no more [no longer] strangers and foreigners [sojourners], but fellowcitizens with the saints, and of the household of God.

The Word "foreigners" is *paroikos.* We are no longer *paroikos,* outside the household, moving around like bedouins, having no certain living place, no definite home. We are no longer strangers, for we are known by Him and we know Him. We are fellowcitizens. "Fellowcitizens" is *sumpolitēs.* All of us born-again saints are God's townspeople. Not only are we fellowcitizens, but we are also of the household, *oikeios,* of God because He is the Father.

> Ephesians 2:20:
> And are built [*epoikodomeo* from the root *oikos*] upon the foundation of the apostles and prophets, Jesus Christ himself being the chief corner *stone.*

"And are built upon the foundation of the apostles and prophets...." That is true apostolic, prophetic succession. The apostolic succession never came through the Apostle Peter. That's a story someone made up, not what God's Word states. Apostolic and prophetic succession including evangelists, teachers and pastors—are for those who are part of the household of God and remain faithful to God's Word. This is God's criterion for special ministries in the Body.

The household of God is built upon the foundation of the apostles and prophets, "Jesus Christ ["Christ Jesus" is the text] himself being the chief corner *stone* [foundation stone]." He is the solid rock upon which we must build our lives. That is what that verse says.

Ephesians 2:21:
In whom [the foundation of the apostles and prophets and Jesus Christ] all the building *[oikodome]* fitly framed together groweth unto an holy temple in the Lord.

There is only one building on that foundation. Those who are born again of God's Spirit, whom He knows as His sons, make up the building, the family.

"In whom the whole building is harmoniously fitted together and it grows..." because new people are continually being born again. That's the growing.

224

And this "...groweth unto an holy temple in the Lord."

Ephesians 2:22:

In whom ye also are builded together *[sunoiko-domeo]* for an habitation [a housing place, a location, *katoiketerion*] of God through the Spirit.

"In whom ye also are builded together for an habitation of God through the Spirit." God does not dwell in temples made with hands, but the God in Christ in you is the habitation of God. This habitation is something that the true God wanted from before the foundation of the world. But because of God's justice, He wasn't able to bring it to pass until His Son Jesus Christ had finished his work. Then it was legally possible for God to have a certain dwelling place within a person when that person would confess with his mouth that Jesus is Lord and believe that God raised him from the dead. What God had desired from before the foundation of the world He was able to see manifested on Pentecost and thereafter, when God in Christ is created in each believer. *That* is God's permanent dwelling place. Now what can we believers do with this creation of God in Christ in us? We cannot feel God. Therefore, the only way God can be magnified is to worship Him in spirit and in truth [truthfully via the Spirit] which is speaking in tongues.

Now do you see why I fervently encourage my people to speak in tongues often? God is Spirit and can be worshipped via our spirit—and that can only be done by speaking in tongues. When we speak by the spirit, we absolutely know that God dwells in us for we show God who gave us spirit.

We have to get to the point that we unreservedly practice the Word of God as the will of God. God, who is holy and who is Spirit, even the heavens cannot contain. Remember Isaiah 66:1 which says, "The heaven *is* my throne, and the earth *is* my footstool." Imagine how immense He is, how great He is! That same God is in us and we are that household of God, that harmoniously fitted temple, the habitation of God by spirit. And whenever we speak in tongues, we are worshipping God, and thereby He is receiving from His children what He worked to bring about from the very beginning. We are now God's dwelling place.

CHAPTER TWELVE

The Final Victory

The great hope of the Christian Church is the return of Christ and our gathering together unto him. There are aspects of Christ's return which we find most clearly explained by God's rightly-divided Word. In order to understand the coming of Christ, we must also understand "the mechanics" of his coming. Jesus' first coming began with his conception and birth and ended with his ascension, over thirty years later. There were many significant phases and events during this time. In this, the second coming is similar: it will also cover a period of time and encompass several significant phases and events.

There are four basic events included in the times of the end, when Christ returns. This is their order: (1) Christ's coming *for* the Church, the Body of Christ, to gather them together and meet them in the air; (2) the events of the Book of Revelation with Christ's coming *with* the Church; (3) the first and second resurrections; and finally, (4) the very end, the final point *[telos]*, when death is destroyed and all things are subdued to God. Having this background, we can now turn to the Word of God and see its clarity.

The fifteenth chapter of I Corinthians contains the basic doctrine about the resurrection and the rising of believers. First of all, we must understand the word "resurrection." It necessitates a rising, but not every rising is a resurrection. Just as the word "apostle" indicates discipleship, not all disciples are apostles. Every rising is not a resurrection, but each resurrection is a rising. This will be clarified as we proceed.

> I Corinthians 15:1:
> Moreover, brethren, I declare [make known] unto you the gospel [good news] which I preached unto you, which also ye have received, and wherein ye stand.

A person can have good news of different kinds. So whenever we read the word "gospel" in God's Word, we always have to determine whether it means the good news of the Old Testament or the good news of the presence of Christ or the good news of the revealed mystery, which is the good news of the epistles.

The words "wherein ye stand" can be translated "in which ye stand also": "Which ye also have received, in which ye stand also." A person can receive something and not stick with it. This verse says we not only receive the good news, we should live it also. So it is a matter of not wavering on God's Word; we must receive and then stand.

Verse 2:
By which [the gospel] also ye are saved....

"By [through] which ye are saved also...." The word "saved" is the Greek word *sozo*, meaning "to be made whole." In this verse, to be saved means more than being born again. A person could be born again and still not be made whole in other areas of his life. When ten lepers came to Jesus, as recorded in Luke 17:12-19, they were *all* healed; but only one of the lepers returned to thank Jesus, and he was made whole. They were all healed, but only one was made whole in ways besides his physical healing. In I Corinthians, God is referring to wholeness beyond what we spiritually receive at the new birth.

"Through which ye are saved [made whole] also, if [when] ye keep in memory...." What are we to keep in memory? All which you also have received, in which you stand also, through which

229

you are saved also. Hold in your mind these things that Christ Jesus did, "...what I preached unto you, unless [except] ye have believed in vain." "In vain" means "to no purpose." "Except ye believe to no purpose."

Verse 3:
For I delivered unto you first of all that which I also received, how that Christ died for our sins according to the scriptures.

The phrase "first of all" literally reads "among the first things." Among the first things he delivered unto them was "that which I received also...." One of the first things that Paul received by revelation from the Father was information dealing with resurrection and rising.

The first epistle which Paul was inspired to write was Thessalonians, not the Book of Romans. Thessalonians was the first revelation written and circulated among the believers. It stands last among the Church epistles in our Bibles, but it was the first one revealed.*

Look at the use of the word "sins" in verse 3. "I delivered unto you first of all that which I also re-

---

*Of course, Thessalonians can rightfully be placed last, because it will be the last experience for the Church.

230

ceived, how that Christ died for our sins according to the scriptures." "Sin," used in the singular form, refers to man's innate sinful nature; "sins," plural, are the results of that nature. Jesus Christ died not only for our sinful nature, but he also died for the results and consequences of that nature.

Verse 4:
And that he was buried, and that he rose [has been raised] again the third day according to the scriptures.

Christ was buried three days and three nights and got up on the third day. An interesting reference to this is found in the Book of Acts.

Acts 2:25 and 31:
For David speaketh concerning him, I foresaw the Lord always before my face, for he is on my right hand, that I should not be moved.
He seeing this before spake of the resurrection of Christ, that his soul [Christ's soul] was not left in hell, neither his flesh did see corruption.

The knowledge of the resurrection of Christ was given to David by revelation. Promises such as this one to King David made it possible for Old Testament people to believe and to walk on God's Word—because they saw the glory of these future events.

231

That is why until we understand the significance of I Corinthians 15, we just flounder around, for we have not the hope of Christ's return. Without this hope we are going to become discouraged and defeated. David, many years before the coming of the Messiah, was shown by God things regarding Christ's resurrection, namely that the person of Jesus would not be left in hell [hades], the grave. "...Neither his flesh did see corruption." If Jesus Christ had remained in the grave, his flesh would have corrupted. Paul also spoke of Jesus' death and resurrection later in the Book of Acts.

> Acts 13:33-35:
> God hath fulfilled the same unto us their children, in that he hath raised up Jesus again; as it is also written in the second psalm, Thou art my Son, this day have I begotten thee.
> And as concerning that he raised him up from the dead, *now* no more to return to corruption, he said on this wise, I will give you the sure mercies of David.
> Wherefore he saith also in another *psalm*, Thou shalt not suffer thine Holy One to see corruption.

This is why I Corinthians 15:4 gives us the account that Christ was buried and had been raised the third day according to the scriptures. This was a fulfill-

232

ment of the prophecy originally given of old to men of God. They saw the coming of Christ, they saw his death, they saw his being raised. The only things they did not see were the mysteries of God, including the Church of the Body and Christ's return for it. All else was revealed to them.

I Corinthians 15:5:
And that he was seen of [by] Cephas [Peter], then of the twelve.

Now, let's begin setting in order the times that Jesus Christ was seen in his resurrected body. In this chapter alone, six appearances are noted. Verse 5 tells us another interesting truth. If Christ was seen of the twelve after his resurrection, then Judas Iscariot must have been present; otherwise, the scripture would have to say "eleven."

Verse 6:
After that, he was seen of above [more than] five hundred brethren at once; of whom the greater part remain unto this present [now], but some are fallen asleep [some dead].

Verse 6 contains the third record in I Corinthians 15 of Jesus Christ's appearance in his resurrected body.

Verse 7:
After that, he was seen of James; then of all
the apostles.

Now we are up to five appearances.

Verse 8:
And last of all he was seen of me also, as of
one born out of due time.

"And last of all he was seen of me also...." His
appearance to Paul is appearance number six. "As
of one born out of due time..." literally reads "as
if I were an aborted one." Paul, in contrast to the
other apostles of verse 7, did not fulfill a complete
gestation period by being with Christ during his
time on earth during the Gospel Period.

The exact number of appearances of Christ during
those forty days after his resurrection I do not know.
There are six listed here, including two appearances
to the apostles (I Corinthians 15:5 and 7). The third
appearance to the disciples is recorded in the twenty-
first chapter of John.

John 21:14:
This is now the third time that Jesus shewed
himself to his disciples, after that he was risen
from the dead.

234

All of these people mentioned in I Corinthians 15 and elsewhere saw the Lord Jesus Christ in his resurrected form. Now in a court of law, the primary witness is always the one who was an eyewitness to a specific occurrence. Everyone else's statement is secondary to the eyewitness. So a man today saying that he doesn't believe that Jesus Christ rose from the dead is no judge at all, as he is refuting the numerous eyewitnesses. Yet many critics or skeptics of the resurrection of Jesus Christ decide two thousand years after the event that it did not occur. It seems to me that the men who were there as primary witnesses should be better able to speak authoritatively. You cannot say that men like Peter and Paul were stupid. You cannot say that all those who went down to see the empty tomb where Jesus had been buried were hoodwinked. They were no more mistaken than you would be had you witnessed a cataclysmic occurrence in your community, and a hundred years later somebody writing about the occurrence claimed it never happened. However, unlike an observation made a hundred years ago or even two thousand years ago, we have proof of the resurrected Christ. Not only do we have the witness of God's Word and men living at that time, but we can prove today that he is alive because we can speak in tongues. This makes us primary witnesses not only to Jesus Christ's resurrection, but to a great deal more. Nobody can prove that Abraham Lincoln or George Washington

lived, but I can prove that Jesus Christ is alive.
Speaking in tongues is also our proof and assurance
of his return to gather together the Church and
it is proof of the future resurrections. This chapter
is going to delve into all these things. The first eight
verses have been just a warm-up. Once we get into
the innermost part of I Corinthians 15, we will see
that there has been a resurrection and that we have
the proof of that resurrection when we manifest the
power of the holy spirit.

I Corinthians 15:9:
For I am the least of the apostles, that am not
meet to be called an apostle, because I per-
secuted the church of God.

Paul's expression here about being the least of the
apostles is an Orientalism indicating humility, which
is appropriate.

Verse 10:
But by the grace of God I am what I am: and his
grace which *was bestowed* upon me was not
in vain [did not prove to be fruitless]; but I
laboured [worked] more abundantly than they
all [the critics of the apostle]: yet not I, but
the grace of God which was with me.

236

Paul said that he labored more abundantly than the critics, specifically referred to in verses 12 and following. Paul was a man of discipline, a man of concern, a man of drive. Today, somebody has to again become disciplined, somebody has to stand regardless of the Adversary's tricks. We have to become much more competent in rightly dividing the Word of God than any of God's critics are in tearing it apart. We have to wield the Word which is sharper than any two-edged sword.

> Verses 11 and 12:
> Therefore whether *it were* I or they, so we preach, and so ye believed.
> Now if Christ be preached that he rose [out] from [among] the dead, how say some among you that there is no resurrection of the dead?

Except for Christ Jesus, all the rest of the dead are still dead. He is the only one that has ever risen from among the dead. That is why it says "out from among the dead."

> Verse 13:
> But if there be no resurrection of the dead, then is Christ not risen.

"...Then is Christ not risen" literally reads, "not even has Christ been raised."

237

Verses 14-16:

And if Christ be not risen, then *is* our preaching
vain [to no purpose], and your faith [believing]
is also vain.

Yea, and [more over] we are found false witnesses of God; because we have [Delete this
"have."] testified of God that he raised up
Christ: whom he raised not up, if so be that the
dead rise not.

For if the dead rise not, then is not Christ
raised.

But if Christ has been raised, then those that are
now dead are also going to rise. If the dead rise not
then Christ has not been raised. The logic is so
clear that it is stated in two ways.

Verse 17:

And if Christ be not raised, your faith [believ-
ing] *is* vain [of no purpose]; ye are yet in your
sins.

Romans 10:9 says that if you confess with your
mouth the Lord Jesus Christ and believe in your
heart that God did one thing—raised Jesus Christ
from the dead—you will be saved. Yet that confession
is purposeless if Christ is not raised from the dead.
That is what verse 17 says and that is what it means.

Verse 18:
Then they also which are fallen asleep in Christ are perished.

"Then they which fell asleep in Christ perished," because there is no possibility of future life if Christ was not raised from the dead.

Verse 19:
If in this life only [alone] we have [are having our] hope in Christ, we are of all men most miserable.

We need a resolution to the hope we have in this life. If there be no realization in the life hereafter of what we hope for in this life, we are of all men most miserable.

"...We are of all men most miserable" means that "we are to be more pitied than all men" because we believed in something that was a lie. Having been led astray is worse than if we had never even considered the possibility of life eternal.

Hope is always used in the Bible regarding something that is not available at the present time. *Hope* always pertains to something in the future; *believing* pertains to those things which can be had immediately. We have the *hope* of Christ's return today because we cannot have it right now. But if one of us needs to be born again, then that person can *believe* right now and receive salvation. That is the way the words "hope" and "believing" are used in the Bible.

Now verses 20 through 28 are a parenthesis. These verses are used as the figure of speech called *parembole,* meaning "an instructional sentence." So verses 20 through 28 are a sentence, a word, to the believers to instruct them. And the instruction is very important.

Verse 20:
But now is Christ risen from the dead, *and* become the firstfruits of them that slept.

"But now is Christ risen..." is literally worded "but now Christ has been raised." The words "and become" are not in any critical Greek text except the Stephens. "But now Christ has been raised from the dead, the firstfruits of them that slept." "Them that slept" are "those who have fallen asleep." Christ is the firstfruits of them who have fallen asleep because he was raised out from among the dead. The word "firstfruits" has everything to do with the resurrection of Jesus Christ.

Verse 21:
For since by man *came* death, by man *came* also the resurrection of the dead.

"By man came death" refers to the first man, Adam. By his sinful disobedience to God he brought death upon himself and his descendants. In order to overcome this, mankind needed a savior. Since man had brought about his own death, it would legally take a man to overcome it.

Verse 22:
For as in Adam all die, even so in Christ shall all be made alive.

This is a sharply divided verse. "For as in Adam all die," cannot be true of the Church to which you and I belong because verse 51 says, "Behold, I shew you a mystery; We [the Church] shall not all sleep, but we shall all be changed." Then the members of the Church to which you and I belong are not *all* going to die. Some will be alive when Christ returns to gather the Church. Therefore, the Church is not going to be resurrected, because to have a resurrection everyone involved must be dead. Since the context of verse 22 deals with the resurrection, we cannot be talking here about the Church. The Church of the Body consists only of those people who get born again of God's Spirit between Pentecost and the gathering together. That is the Body of Christ. The word "all" of verse 22 must be "all with distinction," including everyone else who is not a member of the Body of Christ. It is this "all" to

241

whom the word "resurrection" pertains. In other words "resurrection" in verse 21 refers to all Israel as well as all unbelievers who have died. They are the subject matter of this entire section of scripture.

Not rightly dividing verse 22 has caused all the confusion that has resulted in throwing the Church into the first and second resurrections spoken of in the Book of Revelation. Jesus Christ is the firstfruits, the one and only one who has been raised out from among the dead. But there is a time coming when the dead are going to have a surprise party. They are going to get up. Even those who haven't believed are going to get up. The getting up has nothing to do with their believing; it has everything to do with the return of Christ.

Since not all the members of the Church will die, the Church as a whole cannot be resurrected. The Bible never speaks of the Church of the Body to which you and I belong as being resurrected, because resurrections apply to Israel and unbelievers. The Church of the Body, on the other hand, at the return of Christ will be gathered together. Those of the Church who are dead will be raised and those who are alive at Christ's return shall be caught up together with them "to meet the Lord in the air," according to I Thessalonians 4:17. We will learn more about this later in the chapter. Since not all are dead, this

242

gathering together of the Church technically is not
a resurrection.

"For as in [the] Adam all die, even so in Christ
[also] shall all be made alive [Israel plus the unbeliev-
ers]." Israel is involved in the resurrection of the
just. The plus is the resurrection of the unjust spoken
of in Acts 24:15. This is when the unbelievers are
resurrected, made alive. Now watch how sharply
this is divided.

> Verse 23:
> But every man [each one] in his own order
> [sequence]: Christ the firstfruits; afterward
> [then] they that are Christ's at [with] his
> coming [Israel, not the Church of the Body,
> since the context is that of resurrection].

After what? After the occurrences of those things
which Paul had already written in Thessalonians
concerning the return of Christ to gather the Church.
After the gathering together of the Church, there
is going to be a resurrection.

"...They that are Christ's at his coming" should
accurately read not *at* his coming, but *with* it. And
the "with" is the resurrection *after* the Church of
the Body is gathered together. That is the accuracy
with which that scripture is written.

243

Verse 24:

Then *cometh* the end, when he shall have delivered up the kingdom to God, even the Father; when he shall have put down all rule and all authority and power.

"Then *cometh* the end [*telos*]...." What "end"? The context is talking about resurrection. The word is *telos*. If it were any other word your Bible would fall to pieces. This is like a dog's tail being the end of the dog. The whole tail would be the end [*suntelia*] of the dog, but the tip of its tail is the very end [*telos*] of the dog. When the final end of the end is meant the word *telos* is used. "Then *cometh* the end [*telos,* the end of the end, the final point, the end resurrection]...." In Revelation there are two resurrections: the resurrection of the just and of the unjust. These two resurrections are mentioned in Acts 24:14 and 15 regarding the hope of Israel's prophets. It is also found in John 5:29. I Corinthians 15:24 says, "Then *cometh* the end [final point], when he shall have delivered up the kingdom...." This makes us ask, "What kingdom?" We are not in Christ's kingdom because we belong to the Church of the Body. Who belongs to Christ's kingdom? Israel. He is going to deliver up "the kingdom to God, even the Father; when he shall have put down...." The words "have put down" mean "brought to naught." At the very end all rule of the Adversary, all authority of the Adversary, and all the power of the Adversary shall have been brought to naught.

For the text literally reads, "Death, the last enemy, is destroyed." Revelation 20:14 says, "And death and hell [the grave] were cast into the lake of fire. This is the second death." When the prophecy of Revelation 20:14 has come to pass, then I Corinthians 15:26 is fulfilled. Revelation 21:4 says, "And God shall wipe away all tears from their eyes; and there shall be no more death, neither sorrow, nor crying, neither shall there be any more pain: for the former things are passed away." This state of painlessness will exist after death is destroyed.

Verses 25 and 26:

For he [Christ] must reign, till he [God] hath put all enemies under his [Christ's] feet.

The last enemy *that* shall be destroyed *is* death.

Verse 27:

For he [God] hath put [subjected] all things under his [Christ's] feet. But when he saith, all things are put under *him, it is* manifest [obvious] that he [God] is excepted, which [who] did put all things under him [Christ].

"It is manifest [obvious] that he is excepted..." means that all things are under Christ's feet with the exception of God who "...did put all things under him."

Verse 28:
And when all things shall be subdued [subjected] unto him [God], then shall the Son also himself be subject unto him [God] that put all things under him [Christ], that God may be all in all.

The phrase "all things" means "over all things in all places" meaning supremacy. The Son himself also be subject unto God that put "all things in all places" under Christ that God may be all in all.

That is the end of the parenthesis which began with verse 20. The entire parenthetical statement dealt with Israel, unbelievers, the return of Christ, and the resurrections. None of it dealt with the Church of the Body. Now we are at verse 29 which is a carry over from verse 19: If in this life only we having our hope in Christ, we are more to be pitied than all men. Then comes verse 29:

Else what shall they do which are baptized for the dead, if the dead rise not at all? why are they then baptized for the dead?

Here is a verse which is very unclear in the King James Version. We are dealing with the resurrection and the miserableness and pitifulness of man if there is no resurrection. If there be no resurrection, then there is no purpose to life; we have been lied to. Pagan religions, such as were prevalent at Corinth, often had the ceremonial practice of baptizing people after they were dead. The Hindus of India do it to this day. Yet such a practice cannot give anyone eternal life. Without the resurrection of Jesus Christ, the gathering together of the Church, and the future resurrections, the dead would simply remain dead bodies. Verse 29 asks us why we should be baptized if we are going to remain dead anyway. Now I will give you a clearer translation of verse 29.

> What is the use of being baptized if it is only to remain dead? Else what are they doing who are being baptized? It is for dead bodies if the dead rise not. Why are they then baptized? Also for the dead?

In contrast to pagan baptismal rites which (whether they were carried out before or after death) could promise nothing but a dead body, the baptism of the resurrected Christ is assurance of eternal life. It gives us the sure hope of his return to gather the Church. The resurrection of Christ also gives assurance of the future resurrections foretold in the Word of God.

That is the accuracy of the twenty-ninth verse: "Else what are they doing who are being baptized" has nothing to do with water, but with the teaching of the baptism of Christ within. Christ in you the hope of glory is of no purpose if you rise not. If the dead rise not why are they then baptized with Christ within?

Verse 30:
And why stand we in jeopardy every hour?

If there is nothing to the resurrection, if Christ has not been raised, then why do we every hour jeopardize our lives, why do we expose ourselves to dangers for Christ's sake? Why should the Devil be so busy in his trickery toward us if we are so totally wrong? The Adversary has to work overtime to keep us in confusion about the Word so that we fail to walk in the accuracy and the power of it.

Verse 31:
I protest [affirm] by your [our] rejoicing which I have in Christ Jesus our Lord, I die daily.

"I die daily" means that Paul stands in jeopardy every day.

Verse 32:
If after the manner of men I have fought with beasts at Ephesus, what advantageth it me, if

the dead rise not? let us eat and drink; for
tomorrow we die.

"If after the manner of men I have [delete "have"]
fought with beasts at Ephesus" can be understood
in two ways, and I will give you both ways. Then we
may have to wait for the Lord's return to figure
out which one is meant in verse 32. Either Paul was
literally thrown into an arena with wild animals in
Ephesus, or he refers here to those Ephesians spoken
about in Acts 19 whom he called beasts. I do not
know which one of the two it is. If it is literal, it is
one thing; if "beasts" refers to men it is a figure of
speech. I don't know which it is, but either would
be bad.

"If after the manner of men I fought with beasts
at Ephesus, what advantage is it to me, if the dead
rise not?" Why should I jeopardize my life day after
day if the dead rise not? What is the profit? Let's
be Epicureans. That is the philosophy of the latter
part of that verse. "Let us eat and drink; for tomorrow we die." In other words, if there is nothing to
the resurrection, then let's do as we please. A lot of
people have this philosophy today.

Verse 33:
Be not deceived [Don't let anybody fool you.]:
evil communications [associations] corrupt
good manners [ethics, morals].

Evil companionships corrupt good ethics. In other
words, don't associate with the non-Christians who,
without true hope and not believing in the resurrection, live only for the day. That is the guidance that
Paul, by revelation, is giving them.

Verse 34:
Awake to righteousness, and sin not; for some
have not the knowledge of God: I speak *this*
to your shame.

"Awake [wake up] to righteousness [what is
right], and sin not...." To sin in this instance is not
to acknowledge or recognize the resurrection of the
Lord Jesus Christ: "...for some have not the knowledge of God: I speak *this* to your shame." Well, if
they have not the knowledge of God, they are ignorant. The resurrection of Jesus Christ is the basis of
Christianity. The Church of Corinth, as well as churches today, should have understood this and declared
it to others. Their failure to do this had the shameful
result of leaving people ignorant of the greatest
truth in the world. There is no reason for people
to be ignorant of the resurrection when the knowledge of God's Word is available.

Verses 35-37:
But some *man* will say, How are the dead raised up? and with what [kind of] body do they come?
Thou fool, that which thou sowest is not quickened [made alive], except it die:
And that which thou sowest, thou sowest not that body that shall be, but bare [naked] grain, it may chance [if it should happen] of wheat, or of some other *grain* [such as oats, barley, or corn].

When you sow the naked grain of corn or barley or wheat, it is not that grain which you sowed which comes back at the top of the stalk. It is not the original kernel, but it is new grain that comes forth.

Verses 38-40:
But God giveth it a body as it hath pleased him [as He purposed], and to every seed his [its] own body.
All flesh *is* not the same flesh: but *there is* one *kind of* flesh of men, another flesh of beasts, another of fishes, *and* another of birds.
There are also celestial [heavenly] bodies, and bodies terrestrial [earthly]: but the glory of the celestial [heavenly] *is* one, and the *glory* of the terrestrial [earthly] *is* another.

251

Here is a literal translation according to usage of the text of verse 40:

> And heavenly bodies there will be and earthly bodies, but of one kind will be the glory of the heavenly and of another kind that of the earthly.

Do you know what this verse is talking about? After all is accomplished as told in the Book of Revelation, there are going to be people on earth in the new earth. Because how could a person sell his corn, wheat, and onions if there were no one to eat them? It says in the Book of Revelation that they are going to bring in their produce. But in this new earth there is going to be a little different experience, because in that land there will be no cursed thistles or death. Basically, what we need to see is that verse 40 is talking about heavenly bodies and earthly bodies. One kind would be the glory of those that are heavenly, and another kind those that are earthly.

> Verses 41 and 42:
> *There is* one glory of the sun, and another glory of the moon, and another glory of the stars: for *one* star differeth from *another* star in glory.

So also *is* the resurrection of the dead. It is sown in corruption; it is raised in incorruption.

The dead can be raised incorruptible. You have to be dead to corrupt, and then that corruption can be raised in incorruption.

Verse 43:
It [the body] is sown in dishonour [because it is going to corrupt]; it is raised in glory: it is sown in weakness [because of man's frailty]; it is raised in power.

We shall have a body fashioned like unto his glorious body.

Verse 44:
It is sown a natural body; it is raised a spiritual body. There is a natural body, and there is a spiritual body.

"It is sown a natural body..." because all that can go into the grave is a person's natural body. The body is sown a natural body; but when it is raised, it will be a spiritual body. Nobody knows what that new body is all about. The resurrected body of Jesus Christ was never taken into a laboratory, so nobody knows what that body consisted of. However, we do know from the Word that Jesus

Christ could be on the road to Emmaus one time and the next moment be inside of a room that had the door bolted. I don't understand his resurrected body, but the Word explains this much: there is a natural body and there is a spiritual body.

> Verse 45:
> And so it is written, The first man Adam was made a living soul; the last Adam *was made* a quickening [life-giving] spirit.

When God breathed into Adam the breath of life, the Word says he became a living soul. I know what the life of the body and soul man is; but I do not know what the life of the resurrected body will be except that it will be a life-giving spirit like the last Adam, Jesus Christ, was given.

> Verses 46 and 47:
> Howbeit [nevertheless] that *was* not first which is spiritual, but that which is natural; and afterward [after the natural] that which is spiritual.
> The first man *is* of the earth, earthy: the second man *is* the Lord [omit "the Lord"] from heaven.

Verse 47 reads, "The first man *is* of the earth, earthy [dust]: the second man *is* the Lord from

254

heaven." Instead of the word "from," put the words "out of" because that is the text: "The first man *is* out of the earth, dust: the second man *is* out of heaven."

Verses 48-51:

As *is* the earthy, such *are* they also that are earthy: and as *is* the heavenly, such *are* they also that are heavenly.

And as we have borne the image of the earthy, we shall also bear the image of the heavenly.

Now this I say, brethren, that flesh and blood cannot [are not able to] inherit the kingdom of God; neither doth corruption inherit incorruption.

Behold, I shew you a mystery; We shall not all sleep, but we shall all be changed.

Now the whole focus changes. The text reads, "I shew you a mystery; We shall not all be sleeping." When Paul says "we" he must be referring to all of those in the Body of Christ of which he is a member. God's family today is made up solely of those who are born again of God's Spirit, members of the Body of Christ. It has nothing to do with whether one is a Jew or a Gentile, for God is no respecter of persons. Since Pentecost, a Jew has had no better standing with God than a Gentile. Both are responsible to believe and to be born again to become a member

255

of the Body of Christ. The resurrections pertain to all those outside of the Body of Christ. But for those within the Body, the situation is different. Paul unveils to us this mystery. The revelation is that not all of the Church is going to die. When Christ returns to gather the Church, those Christians who have died will be raised up. At this time all Christians, whether they have been dead or alive, will be changed. The following verse tell us some of this change.

> Verse 52:
> In a moment [atomos]*, in the twinkling of an eye, at the last trump: for the trumpet shall sound, and the dead shall be raised incorruptible, and we shall be changed.

In Matthew it talks about the last trumpet too, but there it is in reference to Israel. This trumpet in I Corinthians 15:52 is in reference to the Church of the Body. If you put Israel in here, you will get your trumpets all mixed up. Why does the trumpet of Matthew have to be the same trumpet as Corinthians? I am trying to show you how confusing and illogical people's thinking basically is because of the lack of concern about rightly dividing God's Word. It is God's Word so we must study it carefully.

*From the Greek word *atomos* is derived the English word "atom."

"In an atom, in the twinkling of an eye, at the last trump: for the trumpet shall sound, and the dead shall be raised incorruptible." It does not say they will be "resurrected" because there are others involved who will still be alive. If the dead will be resurrected incorruptible, what happens to those who will still be alive?

Verse 53:

For this corruptible [that which has died] must put on incorruption, and this mortal [living at that time, not asleep] *must* put on immortality.

Immortality is for a mortal who is living at the return of Christ, one who is part of the Church of the Body. All in that Body will be changed at the return. Those that are dead will be raised and will put on incorruption. Those who are living will put on immortality. Those are the changes occurring to the Church at his return. Suppose Christ came right now: Are we dead? No. Therefore, we could not be raised from the dead, but we would put on immortality. Many people teach that when a person dies he does not really die because the soul is immortal and it goes to God. They are not speaking the truth of God's Word. Immortality pertains only to the time of the coming of Christ for his Church. At that time the dead in Christ shall be raised incorruptible and the mortals living at that time put on immortality. That is beautiful.

What a tremendous reality to any born-again son of God. What a glorious hope! We will all be changed to have a body fashioned like unto Christ's. We will meet him in the air and "so shall we ever be with the Lord," according to I Thessalonians 4:17.

> Verse 54:
> So when this corruptible shall have put on incorruption, and [when] this mortal shall have put on immortality, then [not until then] shall be brought to pass the saying [word] that is written, Death is swallowed up in victory.

Paul has covered an immense amount of ground on this subject. He has told us of the gathering together of the Church, when the dead are raised and all are changed. Previously he has told us of the resurrections which will come to pass much later in the Book of Revelation. Now he says death is swallowed up in victory. According to verses 24-26 this occurs at the *telos,* the final point, when death, the last enemy, is destroyed. But before any of that happens, the dead in Christ shall be raised, and those who are alive and remain shall be changed. Then, after all that and about a thousand years of work, as told in the Book of Revelation, death will be swallowed up in victory.

258

Verse 55:
O death, where *is* thy sting? O grave, where *is* thy victory?

In the new heaven and the new earth there will be no more sin, so there can be no more death. There was no death until after man sinned, as stated in Genesis.

Verses 56-58:
The sting of death *is* sin; and the strength [power] of sin *is* the law.
But thanks *be* to God, which [who] giveth us the victory through our Lord Jesus Christ.
Therefore, my beloved brethren, be ye stedfast, unmoveable, always abounding in the work of the Lord, forasmuch as ye know that your labour is not in vain in the Lord.

God beseeches us to be unmovable. Do you know what "unmovable" means? Somebody said it is like a fellow who steps ankle-deep in cement and then lets the cement dry. Even though we stand in jeopardy every hour, we are always "stedfast, unmoveable, always abounding [effervescing] in the work of the Lord." We just tell it like it is; we open our hearts and share God's truth, "...knowing [active participle] that your labour is not in vain [without purpose] in the Lord," because our labors will be rewarded.

259

Salvation is by grace, but rewards, after being saved, are granted because of labors.

"But thanks to God, who giveth us the victory through our Lord Jesus Christ. So then, my beloved brethren, be ye stedfast, unmoveable, always abounding in the work of the Lord, knowing that your labour is not without purpose in the Lord." Do you see why we can live with an effervescence and a peace; why we can take a stand in our day and time and be steadfast? Because ours is the final victory through our resurrected Lord Jesus Christ.

Appendix

The word *mustērion* is used in the following New Testament scriptures: three times in the gospels, twenty times in the Pauline epistles and four times in Revelation. Not all of these pertain to the great mystery.

Matthew 13:11: It is given unto you to know the mysteries

Mark 4:11: Unto you it is given to know the mystery

Luke 8:10: Unto you it is given to know the mysteries

Romans 11:25: that ye should be ignorant of this mystery

Romans 16:25: According to the revelation of the mystery

I Corinthians 2:1: declaring unto you the testimony*

---

*See Chapter 12, "The Final Victory," in this volume for detailed study of resurrection and "gathering together."

*Some texts read *mustērion*, mystery.

I Corinthians 2:7: we speak the wisdom of God in a mystery

I Corinthians 4:1:   and stewards of the mysteries of God

I Corinthians 13:2:   and understand all mysteries and all knowledge

I Corinthians 15:51.   Behold, I shew you a mystery

I Corinthians 14:2: howbeit in the spirit he speaketh mysteries

Ephesians 1:9:   Having made known unto us the mystery

Ephesians 3:3: How...he made known unto me the mystery

Ephesians 3:4: may understand my knowledge in the mystery

Ephesians 5:32:   This is a great mystery: but I speak concerning

Ephesians 6:19:   to make known the mystery of the gospel

Colossians 1:26:   the mystery which hath been hid
from ages

Colossians 1:27:   what (is) the riches of the glory
of this mystery

Colossians 2:2:   to the acknowledgment of the
mystery of

Colossians 4:2:   to speak the mystery of Christ,
for which

II Thessalonians 2:7:   the mystery of iniquity doth
already work

I Timothy 3:9:   Holding the mystery of the faith
in a pure

I Timothy 3:16:   without controversy great is the
mystery

Revelation 1:20:   The mystery of the seven stars
which thou

Revelation 10:7:   the mystery of God should be
finished, as

Revelation 17:5:   Mystery, Babylon the great, the
mother of

Revelation 17:7: I will tell thee the mystery of the woman

About the Author

Victor Paul Wierwille has spent many years searching, and seeking enlightenment on God's Word from men of God scattered across the continent. His academic career after high school continued at the Mission House (Lakeland) College and Seminary, Sheboygan, Wisconsin, where he received his Bachelor of Arts and Bachelor of Divinity degrees. Dr. Wierwille studied at the University of Chicago and at Princeton Theological Seminary where he was awarded the Master of Theology degree in Practical Theology. Later he completed his work for the Doctor of Theology degree.

For sixteen years Dr. Wierwille served as a pastor in northwestern Ohio. During these years he searched the Word of God for keys to powerful victorious living. Dr. Wierwille visited E. Stanley Jones and studied his Ashram program. Such men as Glenn Clark, Rufus Mosley, Starr Daily, Albert Cliffe, Bishop K.C. Pillai and others were guests of Dr. Wierwille's local congregation. Karl Barth of Switzerland was a friend and consultant, as was George M. Lamsa, the Aramaic scholar, as well as other European and Far Eastern scholars. With these men Dr. Wierwille quested for Biblical enlightenment. In 1953 he began teaching classes on Power for Abundant Living. These

265

concentrated sessions are specifically directed to unfold the Word of God as the Will of God and to answer crucial questions regarding the holy spirit and its present availability and efficacy in believers' lives. Leading men and women from all over the world into receiving the more abundant life quickly consumed Dr. Wierwille's full time, so it became necessary for him to resign his local pastorate. Since that time Dr. Wierwille has devoted his entire energy to The Way Biblical Research Center in New Knoxville, Ohio. There, as elsewhere in the United States and foreign countries, he continues to study, write and teach the greatness of God's Word.

266

X